Portugal

WHITE STAR
PUBLISHERS

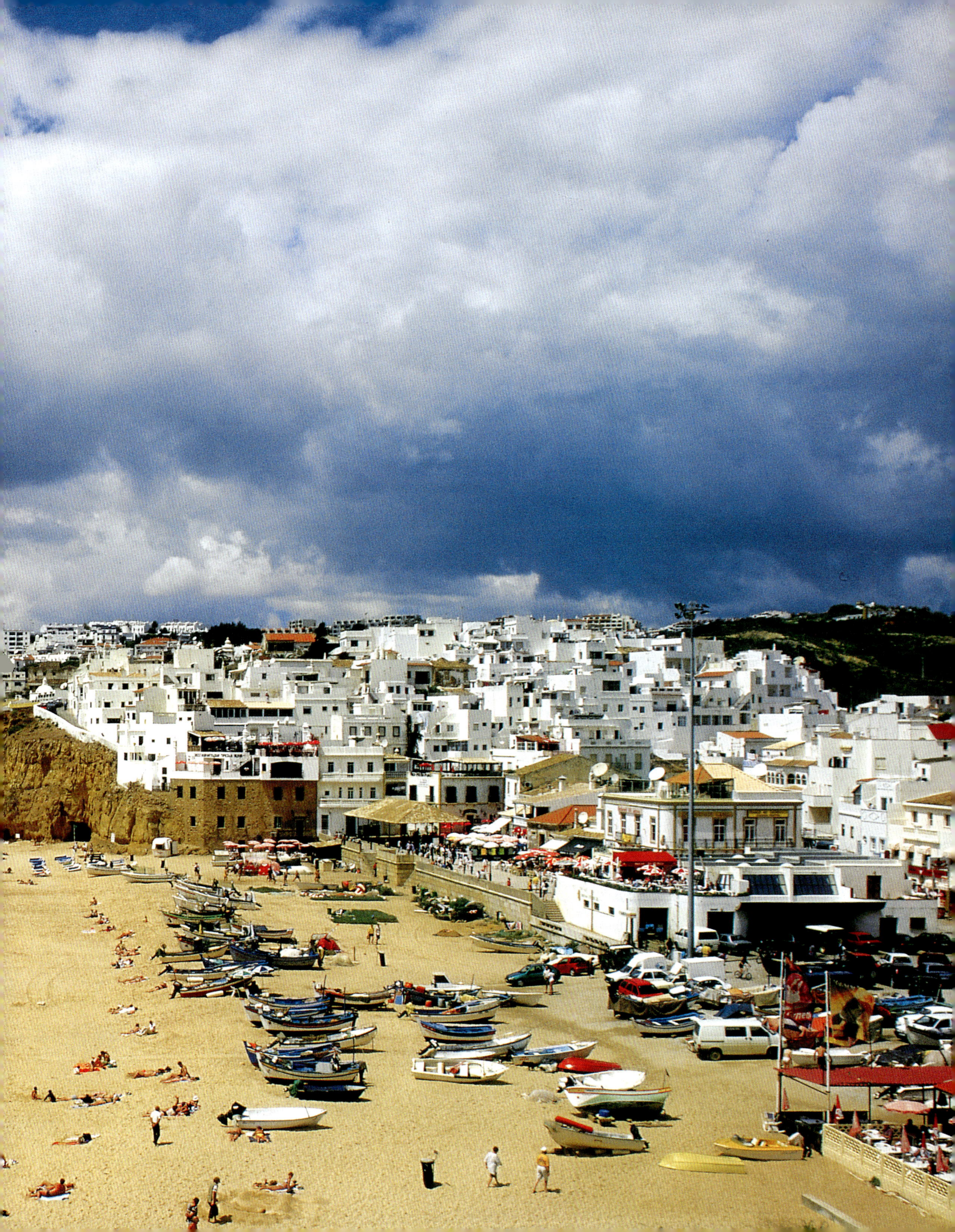

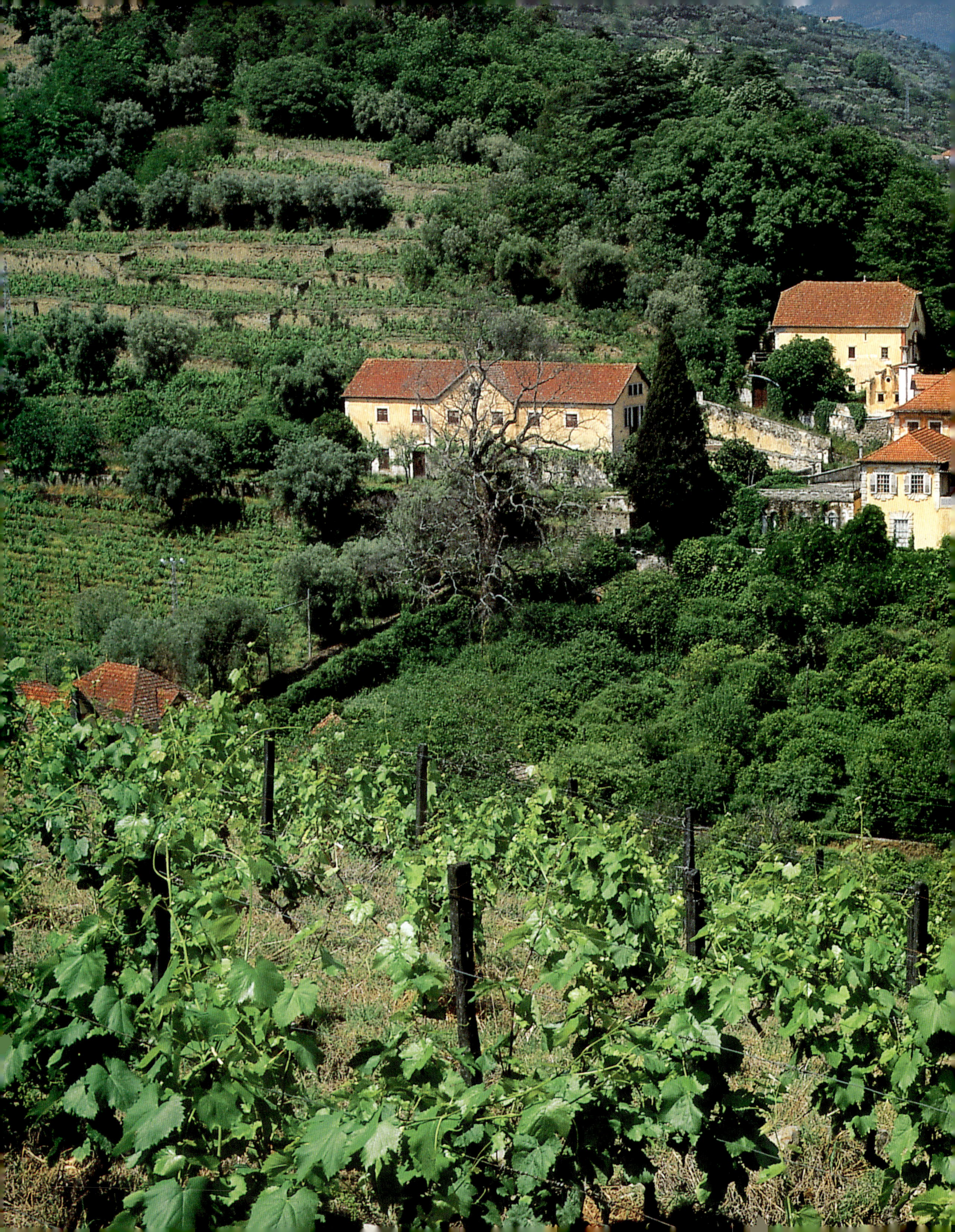

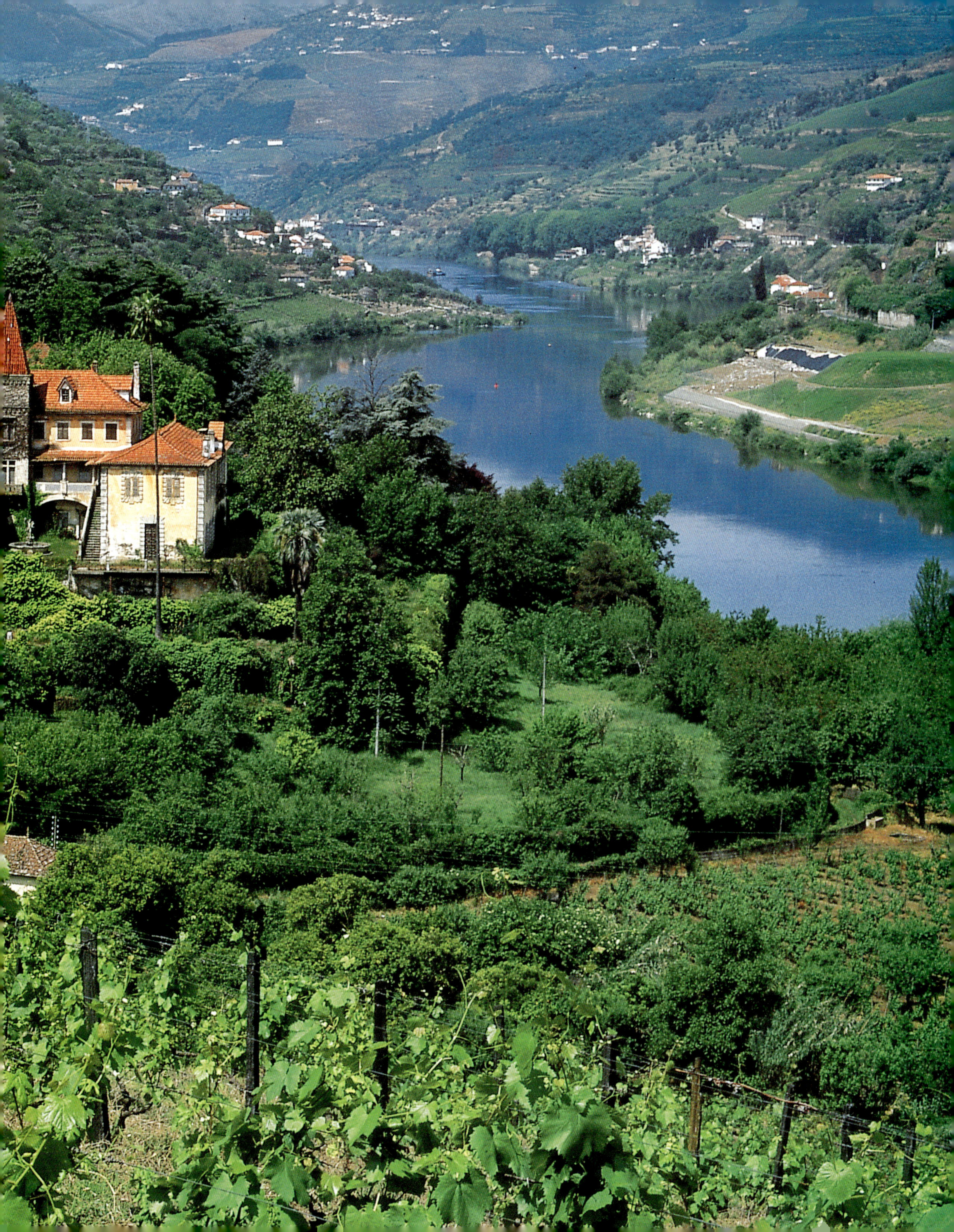

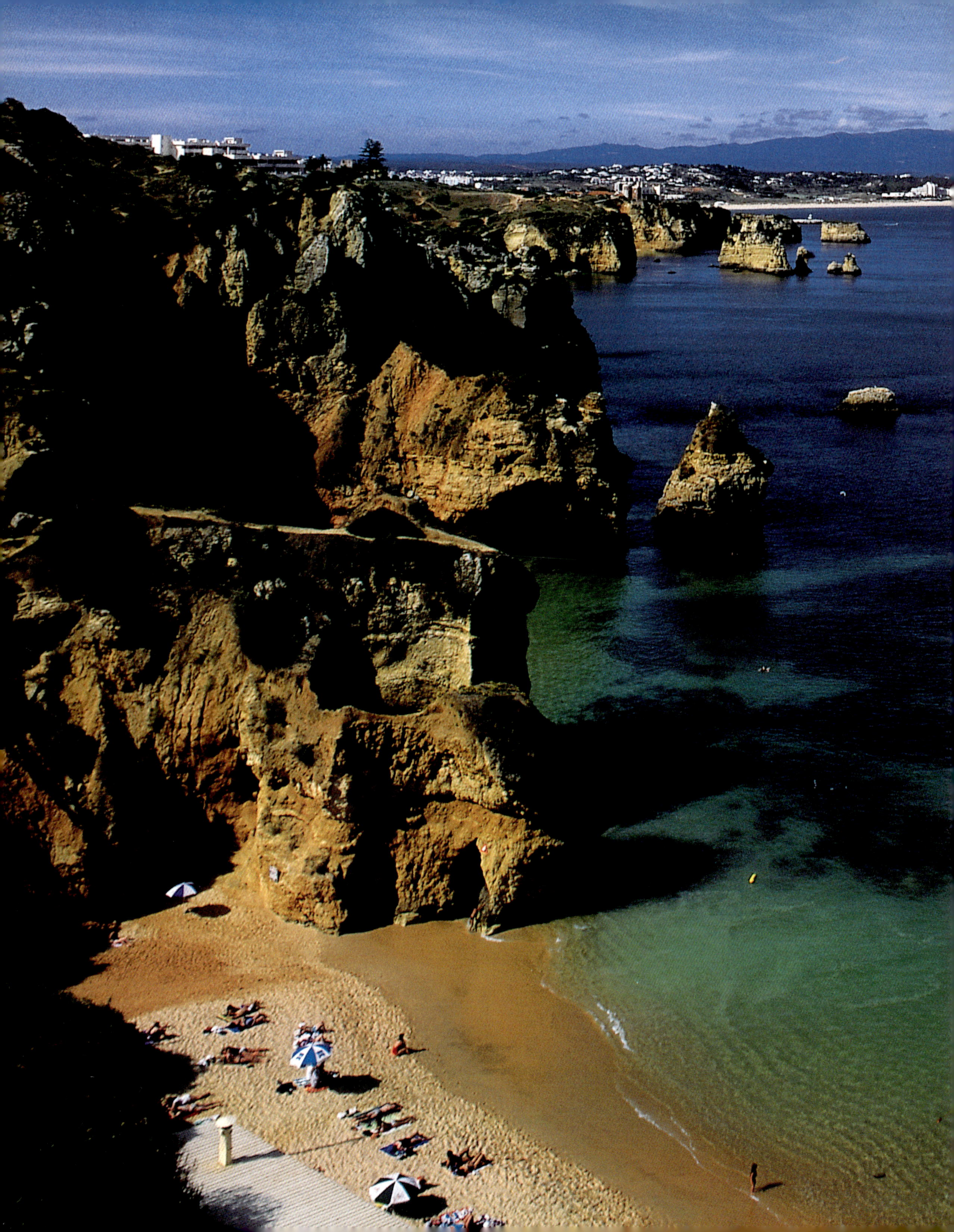

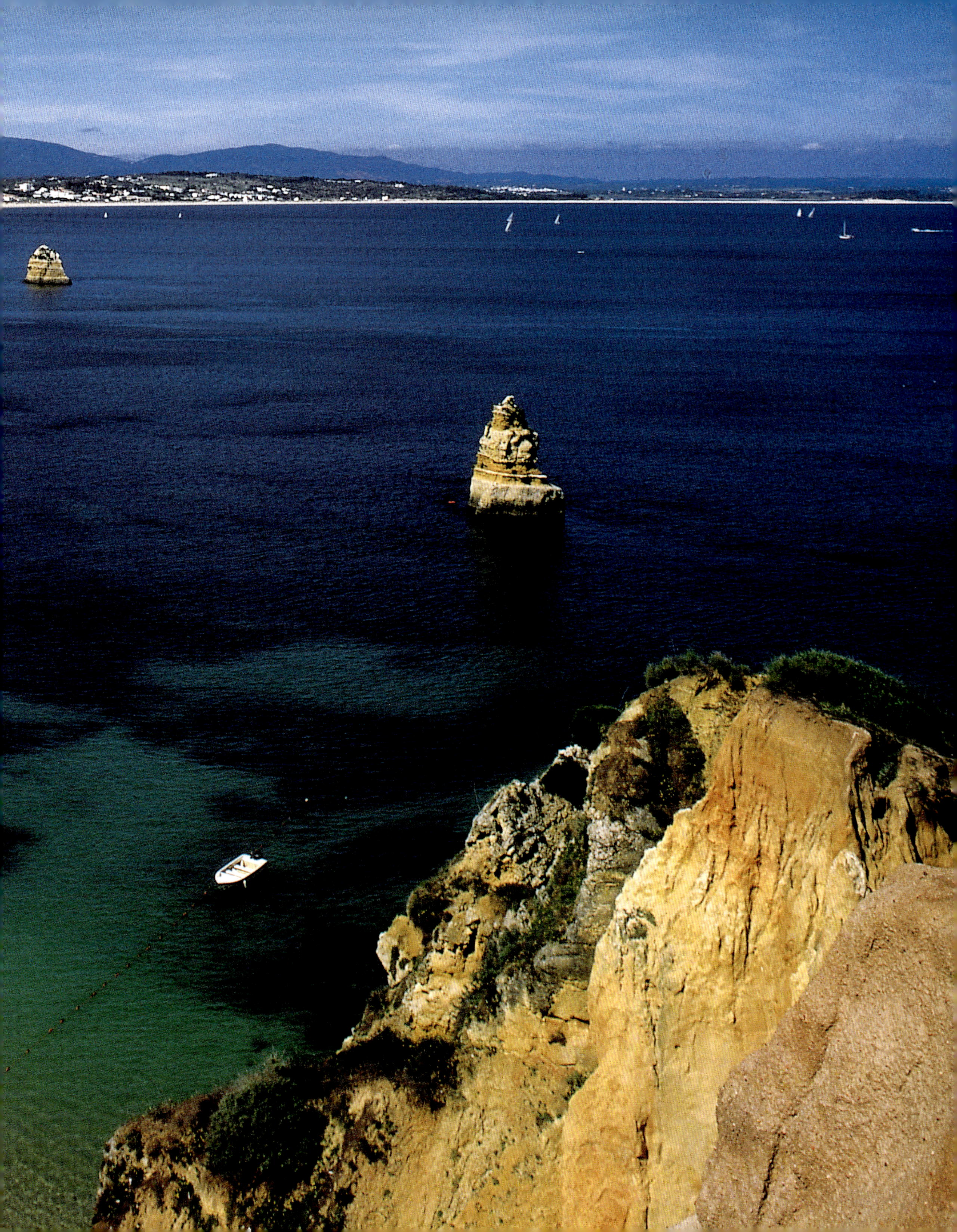

Text
Alberto Bertolazzi

Graphic design
Anna Galliani

Map
Cristina Franco

Contents

Rolling Hills and Golden Sands..........................page 34
The Atmosphere of the Metropolises......................page 68
A Thousand Faces, a Hundred Races, One Soul.....page 106

1 *The grand palace of Queluz is a rococo castle surrounded by French gardens near Lisbon: long used as a summer residence by the Portuguese ruling family, the Braganzas, it now houses a luxurious restaurant, the Cozinha Velha, patronized by Lisbon's VIPs.*

2-3 *Albufeira, is perhaps the most famous holiday resort on the Algarve coast, the ultimate seaside region in Portugal. Despite huge recent urban development, Albufeira has managed to conserve the characteristic Moorish style of the old fishing village.*

4-5 *All along the valley of the Rio Douro, the river that flows into the sea at Porto, the peasants have, over the centuries, laboriously dug thousands of terraces in the rock. They use these to grow one the most famous wine grapes in the world, the only true wealth of this region.*

6-7 *Ponta de Piedade displays the most stunning natural beauty offered by the Algarve: rocks with reddish-golden reflections rise from an emerald-green sea to form spectacular arches and deep inlets.*

8 *The moliceiros are characteristic boats of the south and were, in the past, used exclusively for fishing; now they are also built for the use of tourists. Some are painted simply in bright colors, others are masterpieces with their bows painted in naive style.*

9 *The Torre de Belém is a masterpiece of Portuguese Manueline style. Built on a rocky islet at the mouth of the Tagus estuary, the river that connects Lisbon with the Atlantic, the sea around the tower gradually silted up until it found itself in the immediate vicinity of the shore, where it is seen today.*

© 1998, 2003 White Star S.r.l.
Via C. Sassone, 22/24
13100 Vercelli, Italy
www.whitestar.it

All rights reserved. This book, or any portion thereof, may not be reproduced in any form without written permission of the publisher.
White Star Publishers® is a registered trademark property of Edizioni White Star

ISBN 88-540-0025-6

REPRINTS:
2 3 4 5 6   08 07 06 05 04

Printed in Singapore
Color separation by Graphic Service, Milan

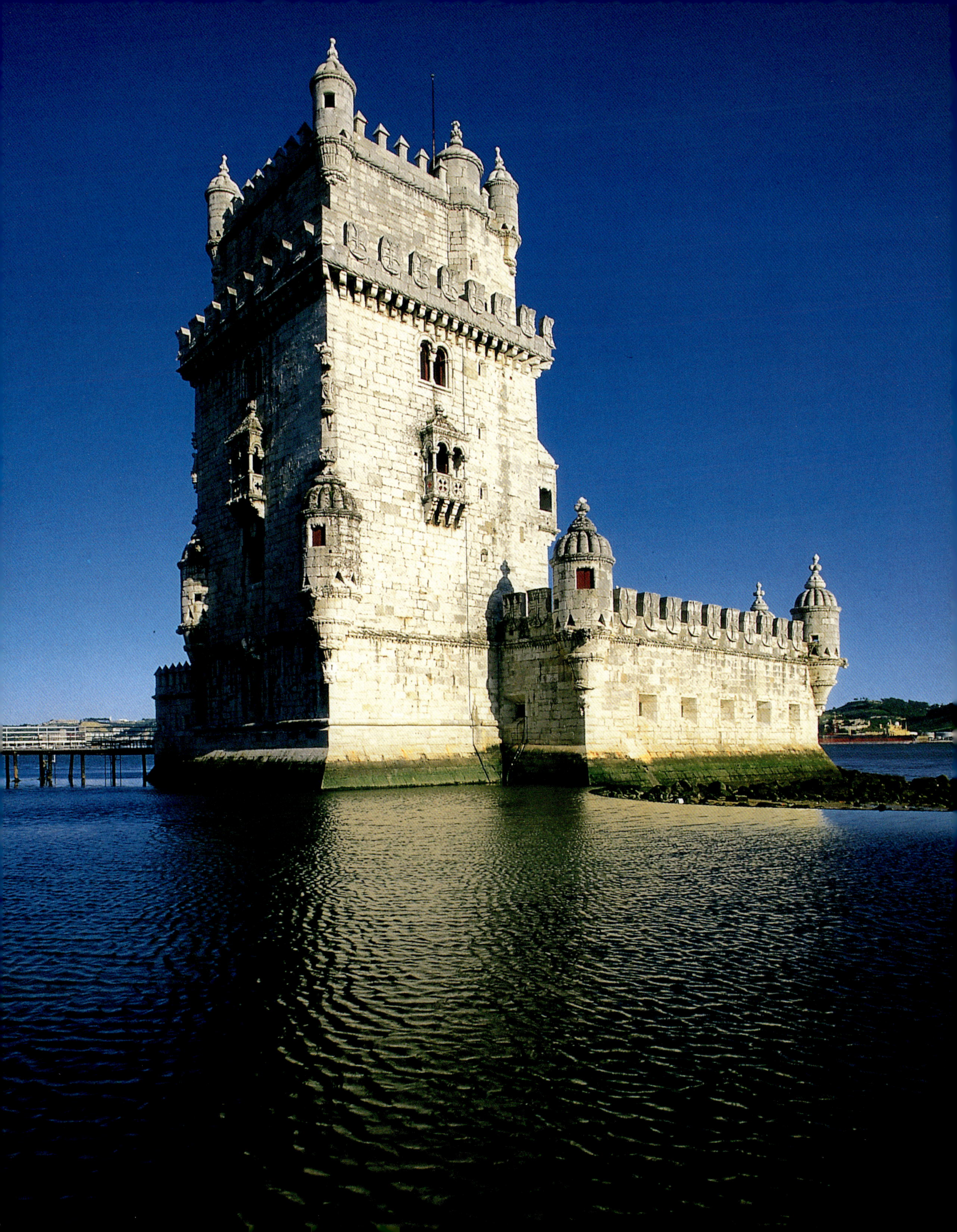

10 top left The obstinate nature of the Portuguese people is shown by the signs left on the land: every tiny patch of arable land has been terraced, even on distant islands. The picture shows Pico, in the Azores.

10 top right Estremoz, in the Alentejo, was a royal residence during the golden era. The castle where Vasco da Gama received gifts to take to the Indies is now a pousada, or hotel, and has preserved its "period" settings and atmosphere to perfection.

10 centre left Obidos survived the forays that despoiled the Costa da Prata over the centuries thanks to its position (raised and inland) and to solid walls that still run all round it today.

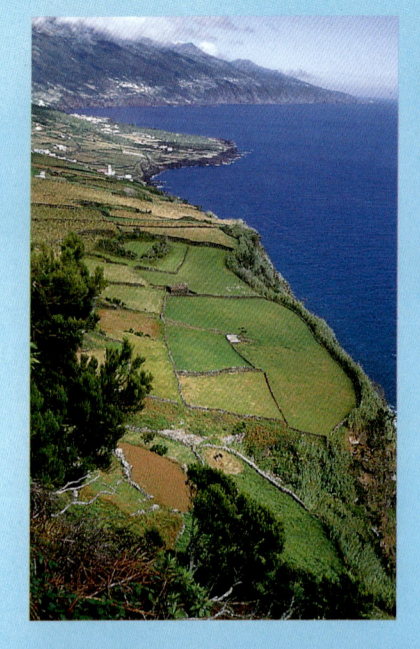

10 centre right Coimbra is considered the "third capital" of Portugal, after Lisbon and Oporto. Its role in culture and research, its world-famous university and its verve make it one of the driving forces of Portuguese development.

10 bottom The Claustro Real, at Batalha, is universally accepted as a masterpiece of Manueline style. In actual fact the cloister, as the rest of the monastery it is part of, is a blend of various styles, with a predominance of Gothic and Manueline.

12-13 The Portuguese have always had to live with the sea. The birth, development and decline of imperial Portugal were the direct result of the close relationship between country and ocean; this is evident all along the coast where entire communities still make a living out of fishing.

14-15 Terceira is one of the nine islands of the archipelago of the Azores: together with Madeira, it is all that remains of Portuguese dominions overseas.

16-17 The Baixa, literally "lower town", is one of the most elegant districts in Lisbon; its "French" plan is the fruit of the reconstruction after the 1755 earthquake.

ATLANTIC OCEAN
SPAIN
VIANA DO CASTELO
Rio Lima
BRAGA
Rio Cavado
Rio Tamega
BRAGANÇA
VILA REAL
OPORTO
ESPINHO
Costa Verde
Rio Douro
Rio Douro
MOUNTAINS
Serra de Mogadouro
Costa da Prata
FIGUEIRA
COIMBRA
Rio Mondego
Serra da Estrela
NAZARÉ
BATALHA
FÁTIMA
TOMAR
ESTREMADURA
SANTARÉM
River Tagus
PORTALEGRE
SINTRA
CABO DA ROCA
LISBON
Rio Sorraia
Mar da Palha
CASCAIS
ESTORIL
ESTREMOZ
SETÚBAL
ÉVORA
Bay of Setúbal
Rio Sado
ALENTEJO
Costa Dourada
Rio Guadiana
BEJA
Rio Mira
ALGARVE
CABO DE SÃO VICENTE
LAGOS
ALBUFEIRA
TAVIRA
SAGRES
FARO
Bay of Lagos
Gulf of Cadiz

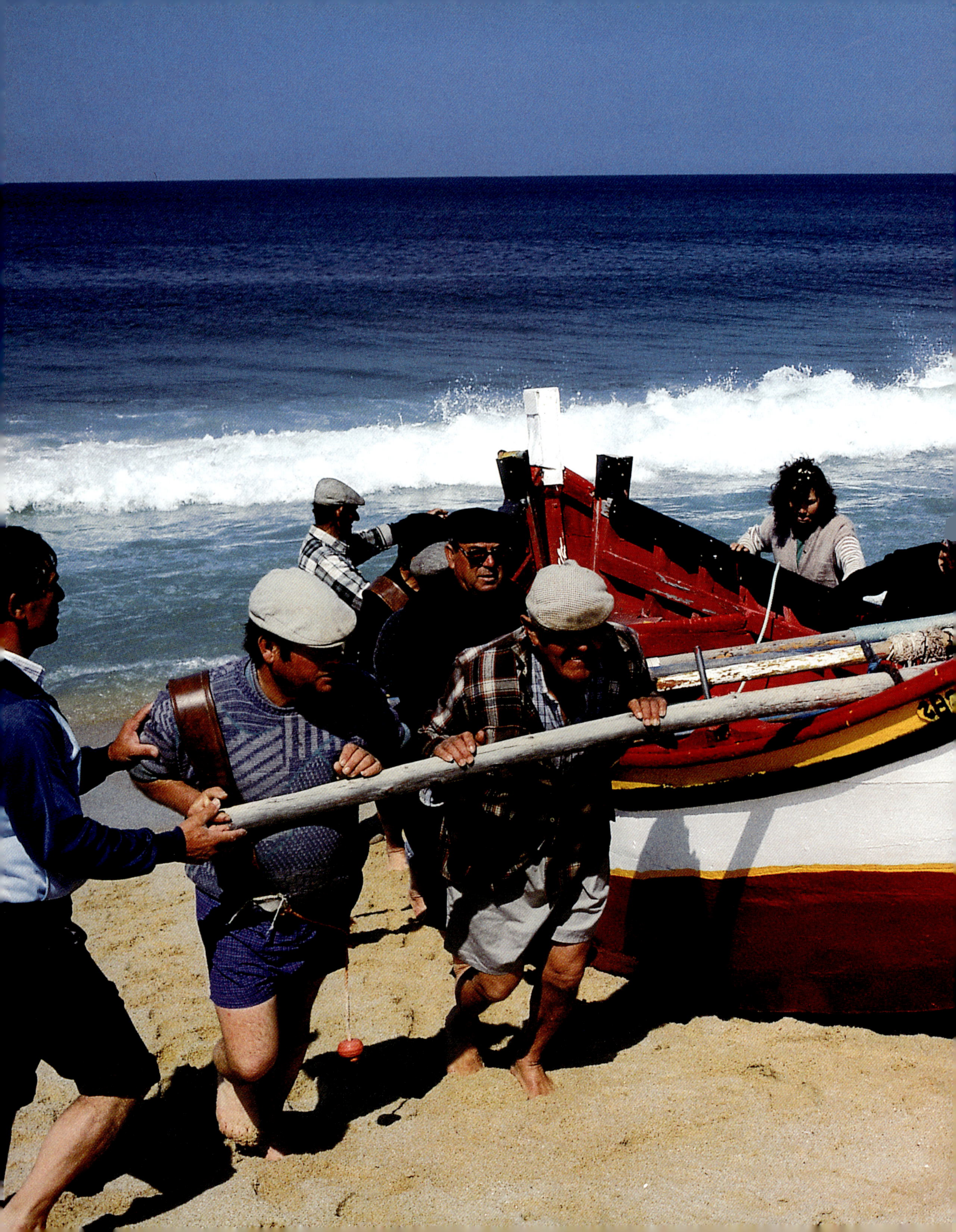

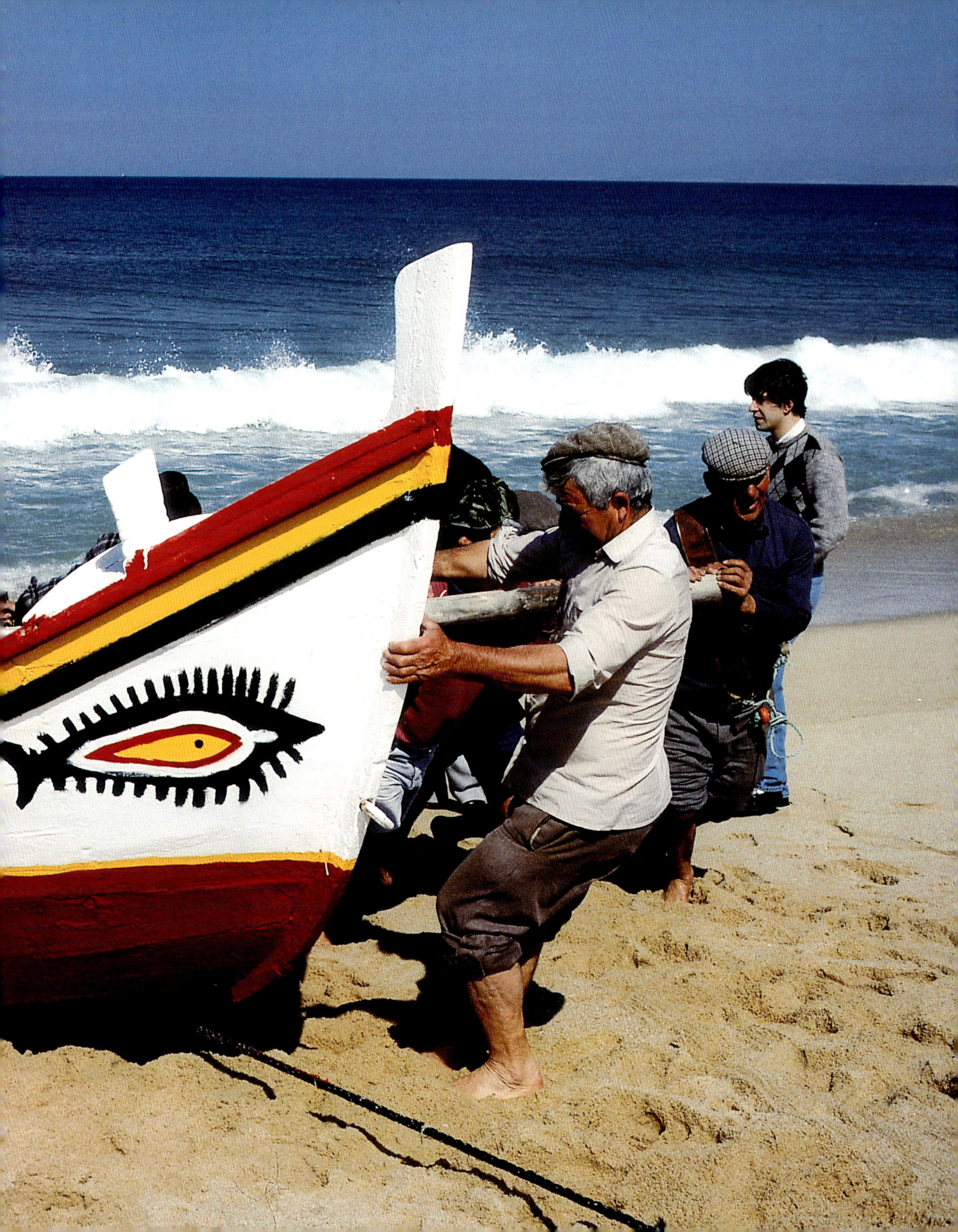

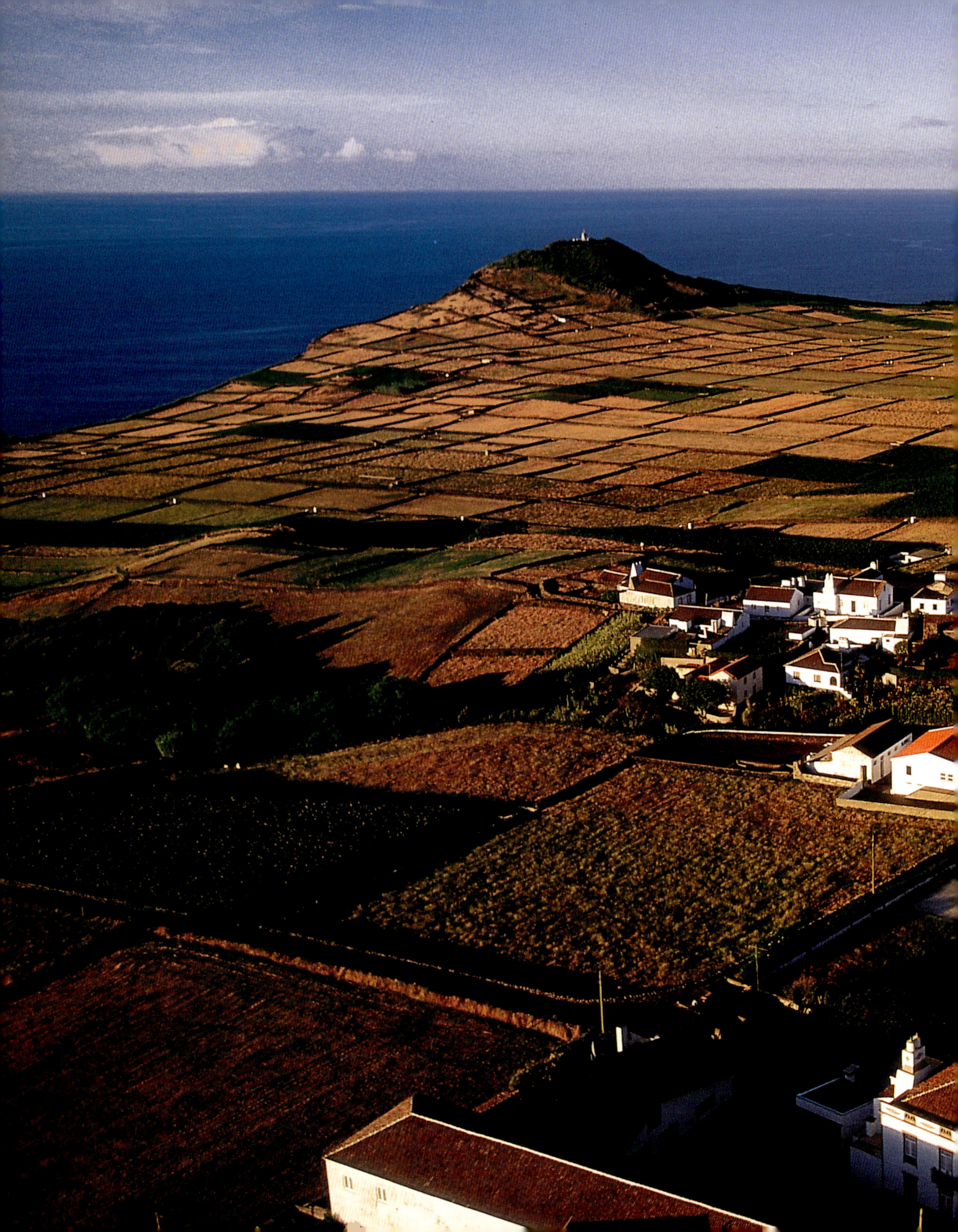

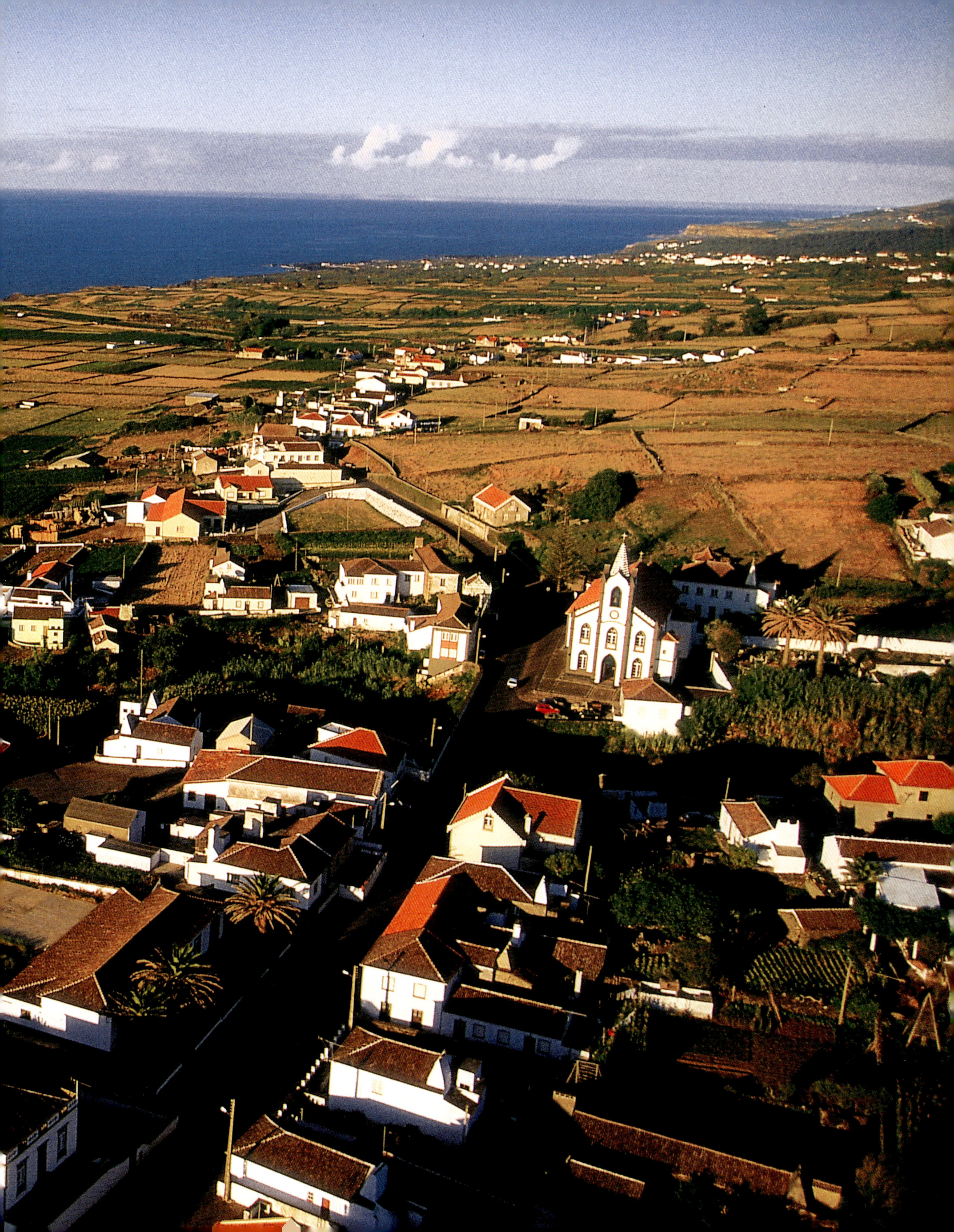

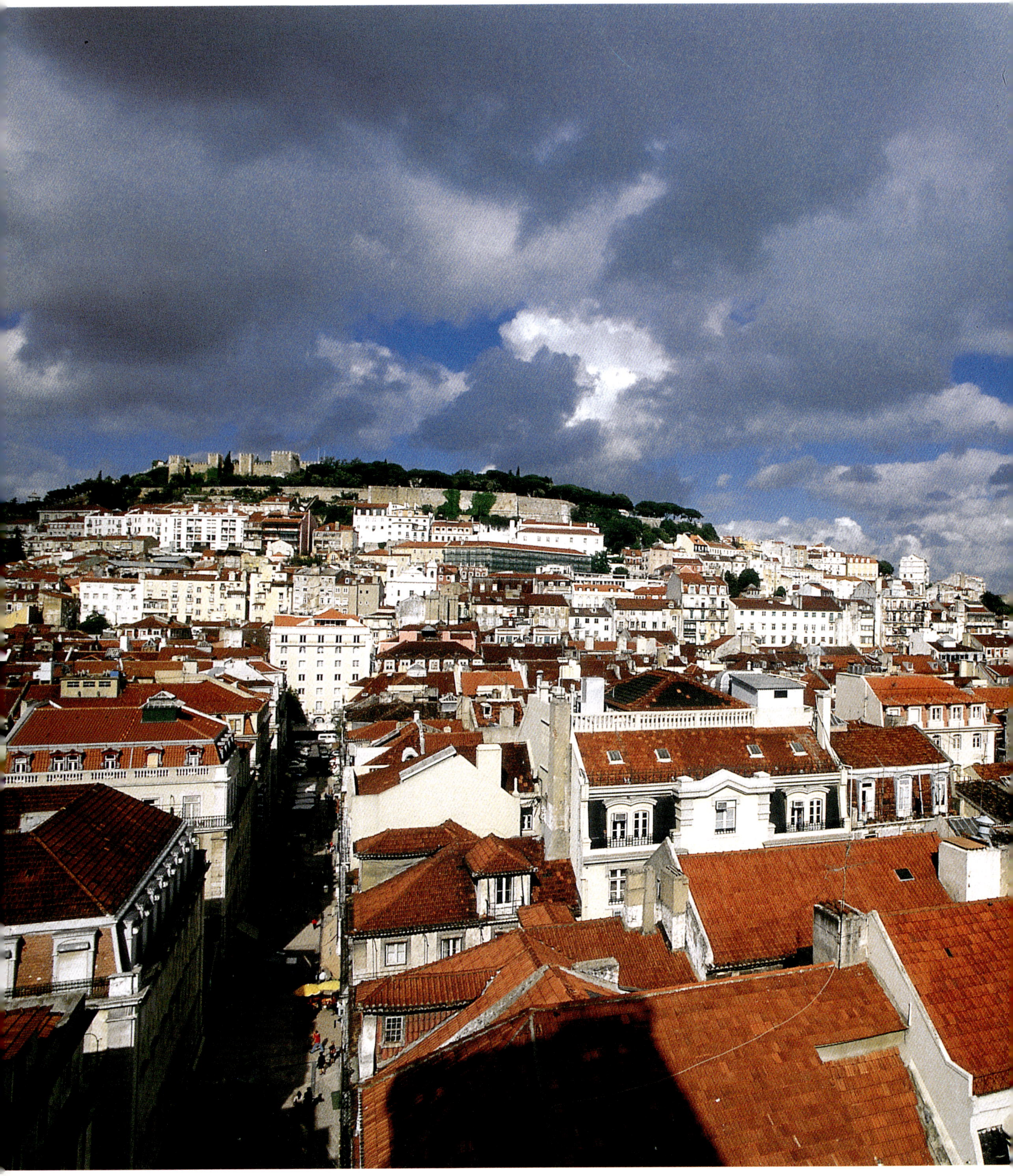

Introduction

On that mild winter's day, his gaze swept over the cultivated Alentejo plain, the land lying "across the river Tagus": all the shades of green were there, and a pungent breeze blew from Spain. That day Dom Manuel would speak to him of a journey that would change the future of Portugal. Vasco da Gama was not yet thirty but he was the leading figure in the school of navigation conceived and run by Henry the Navigator. Henry was a great monarch, of the kind that make history; despite his name he had never ventured farther than Morocco, yet he understood the sea. In his villa at Sagres – built more or less on what the ancients believed was the edge of the world – he had met the best sailors, studied the winds, the known seas and lands, and he had realised that the only way to go was towards the high seas. The art of navigation spoke Portuguese; they had been fishermen since time immemorial, relegated to a narrow strip of land and blocked by a cumbersome neighbour; in that period of the 15th century, the Portuguese were hemmed in.

The fields, those viewed absently-mindedly by Vasco da Gama from the Estremoz fortress, were no longer sufficient: the peasants were starving, the feuds were repeatedly shaken by revolts, and rumours were spreading from the port towns that somewhere on the other side of the Ocean were immense riches waiting to be loaded into ship holds.

It was true that, so far, the great expeditions organised by Henry the Navigator and João II had brought neither gold nor diamonds: just a few islands in the Atlantic (the Azores, Madeira and the Capo Verde islands), a tangle of forests where the air seethed with insects (the Congo) and a headland at the tip of Africa around which the sea raged like the inferno. There, at the Cape of Storms, sighted ten years earlier by Bartholomeu Diaz, the young Vasco was to take wing. In May 1498, after fourteen months of navigation and having rounded what he had renamed the Cape of Good Hope, da Gama landed in Calicut: the route to India was open and with it the rich trade between Europe and Asia was transferred from the crowded and dangerous land routes to the immense oceanic motorway. From that moment nothing would be inconceivable, nothing would be forbidden: and in 1500 Brazil, the most precious (and remunerative) of the jewels on the crown, was "discovered" and colonised.

The adventure of great expeditions that started in the heart of the flat, rural Alentejo plain – where then and still now the peasants' faces, like the furrows of the land, seem incapable of change – altered the geography and distribution of power on earth. From that moment and for nearly three hundred years Portugal ranked as a Great Power; its empire extended to the five continents: from Brazil to Macao ships were sailing loaded with slaves and returning laden with gold; its bothersome neighbour – the great Spain – was forced to capitulate and call for the signing of the treaty of Tordesillas (a forerunner of Yalta) that sanctioned the "bloodless" division of the New World.

The Alentejo and the colonies, rural Portugal and the promised lands, poverty and wealth: all Portuguese history passed through Estremoz, on that memorable day in 1497, as if through a huge eye of a needle. This was the beginning of the greatness and the poverty of present-day Portugal, a country striving to live for the future, gambling on Europe and on technology but never ceasing to mourn a colossal, extraordinary past.

Estremoz and the Alentejo, the granary of Portugal, as it has always been considered, is actually the home of cork: the outstanding quality of the *alentejano* oak bark has resulted in record exports to wine-producing countries (this area supplies two thirds of all the corks made in the world). But the poverty is manifest: the few cars on the roads are either driven by foreigners or are out of date models; the roads are as dusty as paths; the houses seem uninhabited and the shop windows reflect the people's reluctance to spend. Economic development has not visited these narrow country roads nor the brightly-lit, far from crowded, rural villages.

Equally manifest, however, is the inner wealth of the inhabitants. The Dukes of Braganza, who were Portugal's last monarchs, lived here and this shows more in the proud and noble spirit of the people than in the castles and the ancient convents, often now turned into *pousadas* (hotels). In this land, just a few miles from the industrialised belt that runs from Lisbon, via Setúbal, to Santarém, footsteps are slow, the eyes gentle and mournful, the faces tanned and worn and the hands large and hardened.

The landscape, unchanged since the times of Vasco da Gama, has brought this region the name of *planicies*, "plains": fields cultivated mainly with wheat, cork plantations and olive groves, a cluster of white houses at the foot of a castle, flocks of sheep and herds of pigs, the odd bull. Not even tourism has enriched the Alentejo – only the pick of travellers come here, those who want to retreat into the *pousadas*, to relive the aristocratic atmosphere of the good times past, or to breathe what remains of that revolutionary spirit that made this a pre-eminently "red" region.

It is at Vila Viçosa and Évora that the Alentejo conserves the most spirited images of its contradictory past. Vila Viçosa was a residence of the Braganza family, the last dynasty to have ruled in Portugal: their end, which came about *de facto* in 1908 with the assassination of King Carlos I and the Crown Prince coincided with a definitive reawakening from the dreams of glory and the start of the nation's modern history, one of dictatorship and democracy, poverty and rebirth. The splendid ducal palace of Vila Viçosa, with its dimly-lit rooms and cool orange-groves, is a melancholic keepsake of monarchical Portugal, abandoned in the centre of a square renamed, ironically, Praça da Republica. Évora is still enclosed within the Manueline walls: its urban design and the 16th-century university have come through centuries

18 top Tavira is an attractive town situated just over 12 miles from the border with Spain, on the Algarve coast. Paradoxically it owes part of its success with holidaymakers to the 1755 earthquake which produced marine movements that silted up part of the port. Bathers now flock to the beaches created.

18 bottom Tavira is divided in two by the Rio Assêca: a well-preserved 17th-century bridge connects the two quarters, one of which is dominated by the ruins of a Moorish castle.

19 *In Viana do Castelo, a splendid little town north of Oporto just a few miles from Spain, August sees the celebrations for the famous Romaria da Senhora da Agonia, the best-known religious festival held in northern Portugal; for three days pilgrims from all over the country are greeted with fireworks, bull races and costume parades.*

20-21 *Madeira, the largest island of the archipelago of the same name, was defined "part of the world but beyond the world" by Luis de Camões. Of extreme beauty but lying out in the middle of the ocean, it has played host to princes and aristocrats, on holiday or exiled, as well as generations of permanent residents who owe their survival to a little farming and much fishing.*

of decline without a blemish. Only the church of São Francisco and the nearby Capela dos Ossos suggest the by no means quick nor light passage of time. A hanged skeleton serves as the backdrop to this famous chapel of meditation, the walls lined with human skulls and bones; an inscription warns: "The bones here are awaiting yours".

The Alentejo is a kaleidoscope of delightful visions: a thousand colours, as in the wool carpets made at Arraiolos, a village of white houses known the world over for its products of mediaeval origin and flavour; mysterious, as are the ninety-five *menhirs* abandoned in protohistoric times in the middle of a forest of cork oaks at Almendres; virulent, like the *alentejano* bulls – more fortunate than their Spanish brothers, they do not risk their lives during the bullfights: no bulls have been slaughtered in the Portuguese bullrings since Duke d'Arcos was killed during a *tourada,* and their horns are sheathed. Indeed should they suffer injury they are nursed to a full recovery. The Alentejo is the underdeveloped hinterland of Lisbon, the warped reflection of the history, ambitions and decadence of the capital; Trás-os-Montes, Beira Alta and the Douro valley, regions conventionally defined as *montanhas,* are the same for Oporto, the second most densely populated and important town in Portugal.

The barren plains of the central-east conserve the seeds of that haughty desire for adventure that made Lisbon great but the mountains of the north have produced the tenacity and fighting spirit of the most industrial Portuguese cities. "Tenacious" is the only way to describe the fight for survival of the peoples living in Trás-os-Montes, an arid region where icy winds blow for six months of the year and which nevertheless conserves small, ancient communities that live on tradition and stockbreeding: "enterprising" is the only possible definition of the spirit of those farmers that in historical times already worked the hills of the Rio Douro ("river of gold") valley in terraces, creating, despite droughts and with huge efforts, vineyards renowned all over the world. Again, wealth and poverty come and go in these regions far from the sea. On the one hand, men with an unmatched dignity and pride, towns which bear extraordinary marks of history, landscapes of a rare and sanguine beauty; on the other a difficult climate, the hardships of everyday life, unprofitable crops, backward social customs.

Symbolic of the beauty and harshness of these lands, an alternation of vineyards, semi-desert areas, chestnut and pine woods, is the splendid city of Bragança, set on a hill in the extreme north-east of the country. Its citadel is a masterpiece of mediaeval architecture and has survived perfectly to this day; its circle of walls, that can be followed all the way around along the trenches, its well-preserved urban plan, Managem tower and cathedral are the jewels of a unique and little-known village. More famous are Castelo Branco and Vila Real: the former conserves the remains of fortifications, a reminder of the constant contacts between these regions and Spanish invaders, and first-class examples of Portuguese Baroque style (best of all the Jardim Episcopal, the loveliest gardens in the country); Vila Real, as well as for automobile races, is known for the Mateus *solar*, an estate belonging to the counts of Vila Real, who produce the famous wine exported all over the world.

Wine is the most obvious heritage that the Douro passes to Oporto, the city near the mouth of the "river of gold": good quality wine, inexpensive and drunk new, such as the *vinho verde* (green wine), or mellowed, such as port, appreciated everywhere and exported to all parts of the world. *Vinho verde* owes its name to the fact that the grapes used to make it are harvested when still partially unripe; it is produced all over the Douro valley, drunk cool and has a low alcohol content. Oporto is not just a wine, it is the exemplification of the full-bodied and rich soul of the Portuguese people. High in alcoholic content, a variety of blends and *ad hoc* ageing make it versatile and multiform; it can be drunk as an aperitif, a table wine (accompanying humble foods such as cornmeal bread, cheese and olives, or characteristic Arab-Portuguese desserts such as *papos de anjo* or *touchinho do ceu*, with honey, almonds, figs and cinnamon) or for reflection; it will warm stomach and heart, revive conversation or accompany the wistful melody of the *fado*. The port-producing vineyards also symbolise how the Portuguese see themselves: short and sturdy, clinging to the schistose slopes of the valley, they push their roots deep into the ground, to withstand the fury of events and draw up the few resources that a mean land is loath to let go. No storms, snow, gusts of wind or drought will shake these vines, they have always produced tasty grapes which in some *quintas* (wine-estates with cellars) are still trod by foot and this only when fully ripened.

The history of *vinho do Porto* embraces much of the history of Portugal: starting with 1642 when, after a century of wars at sea, the peace treaty with England opened the way for trade between the two countries. Port was officially born in those years, apparently invented in 1668 by two English importers who came up with the idea of adding spirits to stabilise it for the long journey. Much progress has been made since then, yet just thirty years ago the wine was still being transferred from the *quintas* to Oporto on *barcos rabelos*, sailing craft of Visigoth origin that guaranteed slow movement and few jolts. Portugal is an incredible country: nearly everywhere in the Western world manual labour has been replaced by chips and gears but in the Douro valley, during the grape harvest, the men still carry funnel-shaped baskets laden with 70 kilograms of grapes on their shoulders along the winding hills. This toil is rewarded with a little money and much glory. Portuguese wine goes all over the world, but not before it has rested in oak vats for at least three years. The best is aged in bottles, sometimes for forty years, to produce late vintages that are second to none.

Oporto, the terminal for the wine production, is the capital of the Costa Verde, a splendid region dominated by sea and history, as well as a devotion to work. "Coimbra sings, Braga prays, Lisbon works politics and Oporto toils". This old saying is repeated with some

21

satisfaction in the capital of the north, the leading business and second most important industrial centre in the country. With its ocean fog and almost north-European levels of rainfall, this is where the most European Portugal is to be seen, rattling across the Dom Luis I bridge over the Douro river, or slipping from the vineyards of Gondomar into the hard heart of the city – the port of Leixões. Eyes that gaze at the ocean here are not filled with nostalgia: they look towards Europe.

Oporto is not really beautiful but it is intriguing: although grey and foggy for most of the year, it is luminous as only an ocean city can be. Full of parks, it blossoms in spring like a Mediterranean metropolis, smelling of grapes and salt. Just one true "seamen's" district remains: Ribeira, a tangle of narrow streets and houses overlooking one another, damp and, for the most part, crumbling; quaint and alarming because they have not yet been abandoned, indeed they are very much alive. The shops, as noisy as an Oriental market, the smells, bitter and subtle as befits a seafaring village, the poor people, who have not yet been evicted from the houses of an old city centre that attracts no building speculators, are a common sight in Genoa, Naples, Palermo, Barcelona, Marseilles, Athens and Lisbon too: all great seafaring cities that do not disown their history, bound to fishing and hence to hunger.

But the history of Oporto is also one of industry and trade, and so wealth. This is visible in its Baroque churches: from that of São Francisco, with its typically opulent gilded carvings made in 1753 using nearly 500 pounds of gold from the Brazilian colony, to the Igreja dos Clerigos, built at the height of the city's splendour in the 18th century, to an oval plan and with the highest bell-tower in Portugal (the Torre dos Clerigos, 250 feet high with 225 steps).

The new wealth can be perceived in the shops that line the streets of the old centre, where the mediaeval tradition of streets "specialised" in just one trade persists, and in some of the city restaurants, including those serving *dobrada a moda do Porto* (simply veal tripe, chicken and beans) which is not a humble dish, but a regional gastronomic masterpiece. With a touch of snobbery perhaps, the city's VIPs will meet at the O Tripeiro (tripe restaurant) rather than O Escondidinho and prefer what used to be the food of the poor to the squid, oysters, salmon and lobster normally served here.

A taste of well-being can also be had along the Miramar beach or at Espinho, with its modern luxury hotels and numerous golf clubs, or a few miles farther north at the ocean port of Viana do Castelo; here busy shipyards, a fishing fleet, aristocratic villas dating from the late-Manueline period, a square – Praça da Republica – of rare beauty and the original iron-bridge designed by Eiffel give the visitor the impression of something more than an elegant seaside resort. The Costa Verde is also a treasure chest of natural wealth in recent years turned to account for tourism. The countryside, green as the name of the region suggests, benefits from plentiful rainfall and presents a charming alternation of hills and plains, chestnut woods and open valleys, cultivated with vines

22 top *Every year more than a million pilgrims come from all over the world to visit the sanctuary of Fátima. The pilgrimage season starts officially in the middle of May and ends around mid-October. By tradition the first and last pilgrimages are the most crowded.*

22 bottom *The Alentejo ("the land across the river Tagus") is considered the granary of Portugal. Actually it is, above all, the region of corks; the cultivation of oak trees has made this region the world's leading cork exporter: more than two thirds of all the wine corks purchased on the five continents originate here.*

and dotted with small country houses in granite. The coast is still intact, lined with beaches of fine sand, on which the seaside amenities are often hidden – as at Praia do Ofir – between the ocean-side dunes and pinaster woods.

The sea does not only symbolise Portugal's past. Beaches of fine Atlantic sand are scattered along the Costa de Prata, descending towards Lisbon, and give a more distinctive imprint to the south of the country. Inland, along the road between two "capitals", that of the north and that of the south, is the third, Coimbra. Once the administrative capital, today it is a capital of culture – for its ancient university – and of the *fado*. Beautiful and elegant as at Nazaré, with its fishermen and splendid unadulterated beaches (a picture postcard famous the world over) the Costa da Prata is not a "riviera" in the seaside sense of the word: it does not resemble the Algarve, a land of tourism, warm Mediterranean winds and lush vegetation. It is the epitome of coastal Portugal: harsh and gentle, refined and common, beaten by the ocean winds in winter and a tropical sun in summer. The beaches, some refined such as those of Estoril and Cascais, two of the most famous resorts on the south coast, are crowded nonetheless. Estoril, renowned for its famous casino and sumptuous villas hidden by vegetation, is perhaps the most elegant seaside resort; Cascais, although no longer a fishing village, conserves the traits of a small seafaring village – low brightly-coloured houses, narrow streets, bars and restaurants on the sea shore. High-class houses and gardens have brought prestige to Benfica, one of the capital's old suburbs, famous for the Palácio do Marques de Fronteira, a lovely 17th-century villa with two splendid period gardens, and for the huge stadium that hosts the exploits of Lisbon's leading football team, one of the most blazoned in Europe. Pomp and splendour also shine at Queluz, in the summer residence of the royal household, the "Versailles of Portugal", and at Sintra which possesses the country's most extraordinary castle, the Castelo da Pena. Remarkable and impressive is the section of the Aqueduto das Aguas Livres that crosses the Alcantara valley: it took more than three hundred years to complete and thus resolve the capital's eternal problem: lack of water.

From the small towns to Lisbon is no short leap. Although the countryside and seafaring villages have provided the Portuguese capital with manpower since the Middle Ages, Lisbon is today a cosmopolitan city, overcrowded and bewildering, where the pace is fast and minutes count. Lisbon is a city of a thousand faces; the westernmost European capital, it is firmly anchored to the continent but turned always to the Atlantic. Its survival was long bound to its two seas: the Mar de Palha, "Sea of Straw", formed by the wide mouth of the Tagus river, and the Atlantic Ocean, ploughed by caravels and galleons, fishing boats and whalers. Lisbon conserves the fascination of what was once the maritime capital of the post-Renaissance world: the *ruas*, narrow alleyways common to seafaring towns, the low, brightly-lit coloured houses of Alfama or Belém, the fragrant Arab-style squares and the wide *avenidas*,

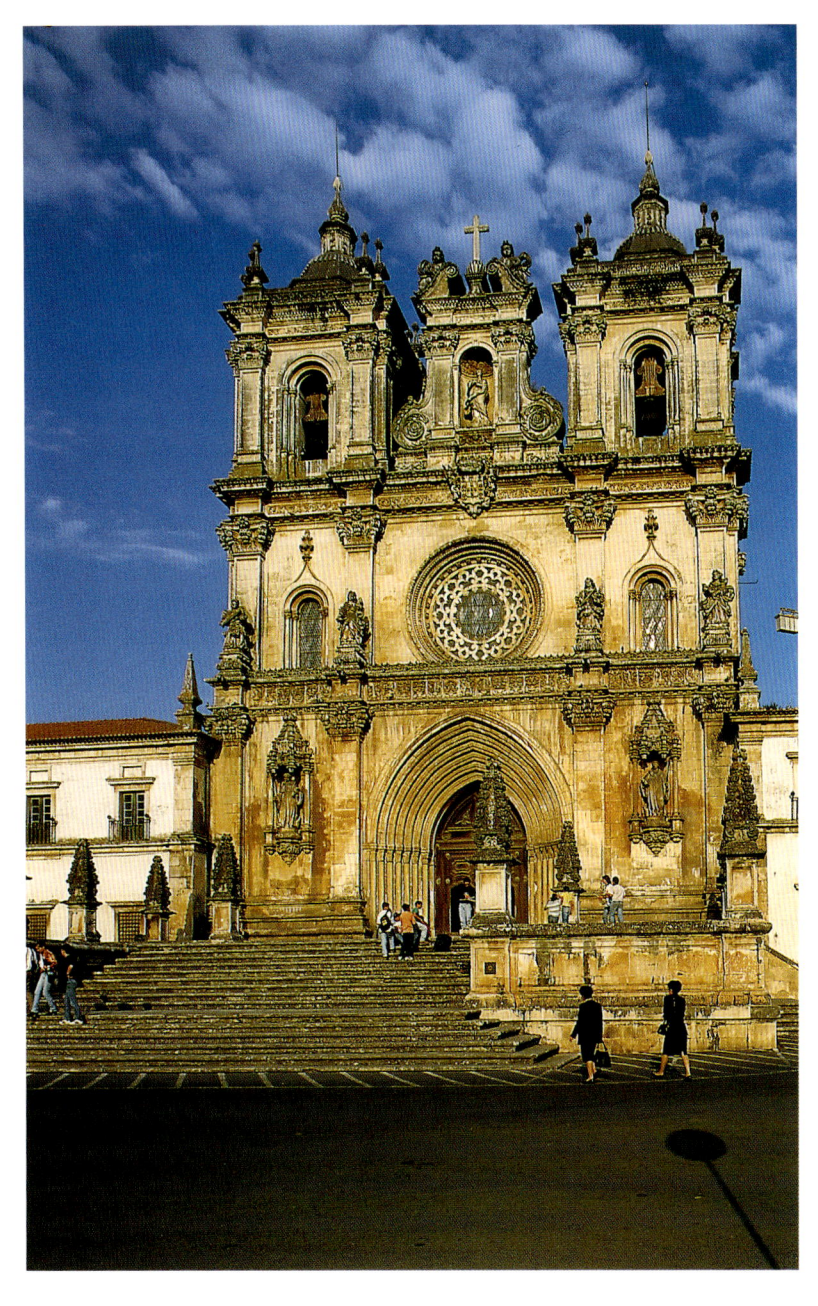

23 *On the main square of Alcobaça, a little town inland of the Costa da Prata famous for its wines and liqueurs, stands the splendid Abbey of Santa Maria, a monastery founded by the Cistercians in the middle of the 12th century. Interesting visits can be made to the huge kitchens, the so-called "cloister of silence" and the tombs of Pedro I and Inés de Castro.*

24-25 *The university of Coimbra is the most important in the country and one of the most famous in the world. Its library is a fine example of early 18th-century Baroque architecture. The ceilings feature much tromp l'oeil, a technique borrowed from the great French mansions and applied here with the use of rich materials (gold, wood, marble), and stucco-work; most of the decorations are inspired by the exploits of imperial Portugal, with references to the colonial dominions on the five continents. The immense library archives also conserve precious mediaeval works.*

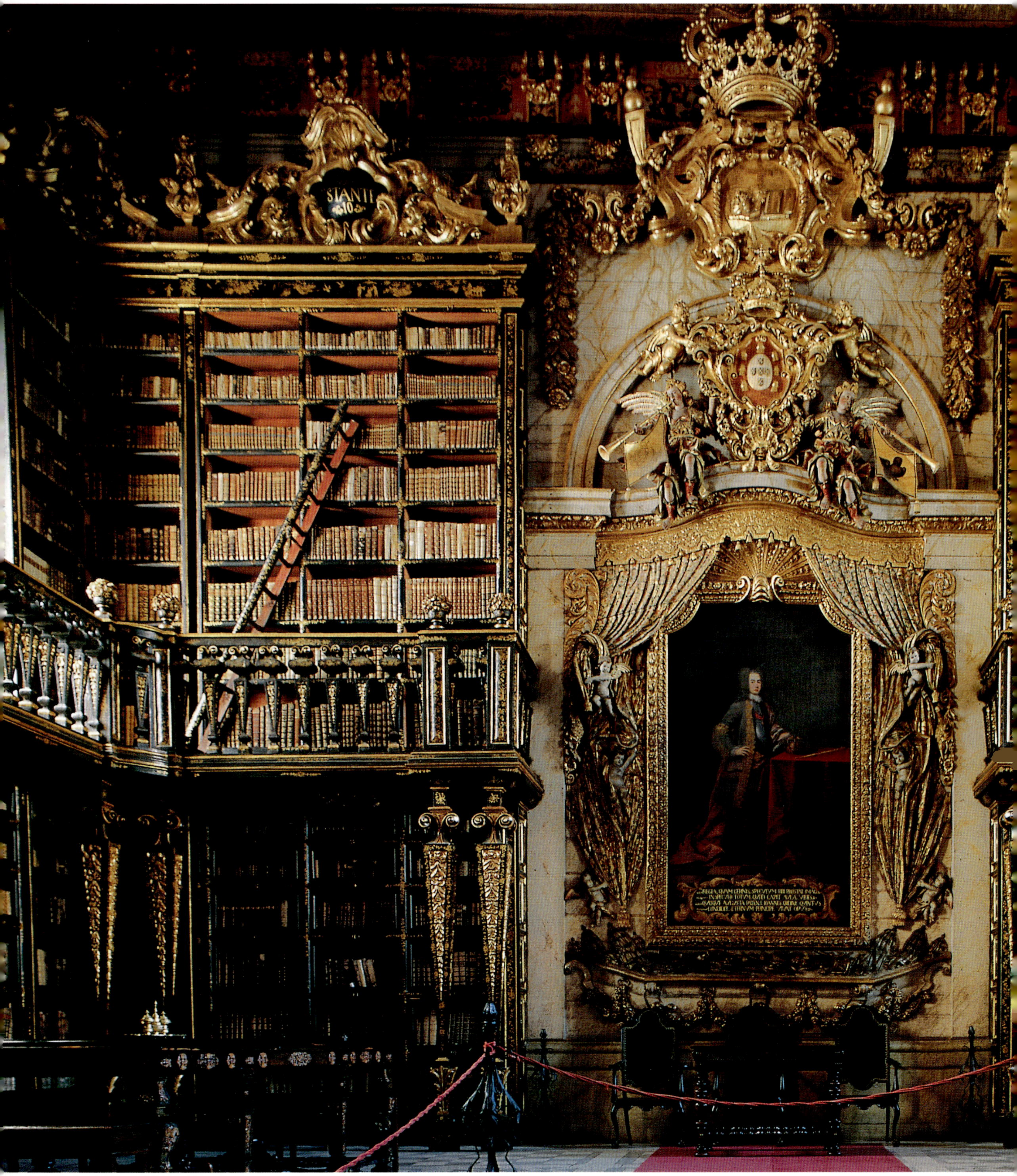

the 18th-century palaces of the Baixa and the immense gardens that surround the loveliest *praças* (squares). The charm of Lisbon lies also in the beauty of the bay before it, in the Atlantic mists and fresh water of the Tagus river that originates in Spain and flows into the ocean from a strange bulb-shaped mouth. On the vast northern shores of this lagoon (called "Sea of Straw" for its golden reflections), amidst hills sloping from the Estremadura and the waters of the Tagus, is the loveliest part of Lisbon. Crossed on the *electricos*, the picturesque trams that trudge up and down its streets, seen from the *elevador*, unusual lifts that link the lower and upper city, or admired from the ferries that connect it to the southern shore, the historic centre of the capital is both luminous and intriguing, sweet and solemn; the view from the castle of São Jorge, down on the Praça do Comércio, the coloured houses and the gardens of Belém as far as the interminable Ponte 25 Abril brings an old Portuguese proverb to mind that says "*Quem nao tem visto Lisboa, nao tem visto cousa boa*" (He who has not seen Lisbon, has never seen beauty").

For its historical ups and downs and for the melting pot of cultures it has raised, Lisbon is many cities in one. Every district possesses a sort of biological impression: the Bairro Alto and Alfama preserve the traces of the Muslim passage and present the most cheerful and boisterous signs of everyday life; the Baixa, Rossio, Chiado and the Praça do Comércio, fashioned by the aristocratic and wealthy hand of ancient Portuguese nobility, reflect the elegance of good times past. Diversity is one of its most obvious traits and is best condensed in the Manueline style, a mixture of the most varied artistic forms, of sea, epic, sacred and profane motifs, all held together by a proud and daring love of conquest and discovery.

The inhabitants of Lisbon remember with great sorrow the event which, to their minds, changed the history of the city and that of all Portugal: on All Saint's Day 1755 an earthquake razed much of the city to the ground and a sixth of the population was buried under the ruins. Until that moment the glory of Lisbon and that of Portugal had been one: as Paris for France or London for England, the city was the whole nation. It was a long journey, from the Phoenicians – who had founded it as *Alis Ubbo* ("sweet bay") to the Arabs – who renamed it *al-Aschbouna*, and contributed towards its Oriental appearance, clearly visible in all the districts bearing an Arab name (Alfama, Alcantara, Mouraria) – to the mythical gold era sung by the poet Luís Camões and immortalised in inimitable monuments. But the decline of the maritime empires was just around the corner: the calamity that struck in the middle of the 18th century may have wounded the Portuguese soul and changed the civil structure of Lisbon more than it actually affected the history of Portugal. It was a historic coincidence of strong symbolical rather than practical value. The reconstruction, costly and rapid, guided by the Portuguese Richelieu, the Marques de Pombal, showed that it was not the public coffers that were spent, in that ruinous 18th century, but the colonial experience, and with it the survival of maritime powers that had failed at home to create an economic structure that would integrate the exploitation of overseas possessions. Portugal was not England, which imported from its colonies the raw materials that fuelled the industrial revolution. The country, in the late 1700s, was falling behind the times and missing the opportunity for new wealth.

The decline of the Portuguese empire has left the magnificent beauty of the squares built by Pombal and the completely rebuilt Baixa district. Nothing has changed in the Portuguese capital since the time of that huge urban rethinking, save for the recent economic boom and its symbols, the skyscrapers and shopping centres that have sprung up in the suburbs. The oldest Lisbon, a port-city of a clearly Arab imprint, no longer really exists. Substantial traces have been preserved, especially in the Alfama, the old district of the Moors and prostitutes – a tangle of streets and alleys, washing hung out between one house and another and tiny squares. Having survived the earthquake, thanks perhaps to the thermal system that serves as a foundation to its houses and which probably gave it its name (*al-Hama*, thermal springs), Alfama lies on the slope that descends from São Jorge towards the Tagus. In the Middle Ages the notables of Lisbon lived there; later it became a residential quarter, first Arab, then Jewish, finally of fishermen and tradesmen. In the times of Pombal it had become a "ghetto" of prostitutes and sailors, a breeding ground for disease that Pombal himself would have razed to the ground. Today, the non-improvement works for the tourist industry; cleansed of its bacteria, Alfama retains the strong fragrances and cries of the people in the small shops that open onto the alleys, large pots of rubber plants at the corners of the squares, ancient fountains (such as the Chafariz d'el Rei), the oldest church in Lisbon (Sé Patriarcal), the most unusual private building (Casa dos Bicos, with a diamond-pointed stone façade) and the most genuine spirit of the people embodied in the Feira da Ladra, the flea market of Campo de Santa Clara, where shoppers are often swindled but also find excellent bargains.

The other three cardinal points of Lisbon are Praça do Comércio, the Rossio and the Baixa. Praça do Comércio, or Terreiro do Praço, is practically a terrace with a small flight of steps extending towards the Tagus and affording views of the Atlantic: it is one of the loveliest squares in Europe, according to those who have visited it over the centuries, from Byron to Mann. The Rossio, officially the Praça de Dom Pedro IV, is airy and vibrant: it is the scene of the *movida* (night-life) of Lisbon, partly thanks to the Teatro Nacional Dona Maria II, one of the hubs of society life.

The Baixa, the lower town destroyed by the earthquake, was redesigned by Pombal to the architectural standards in vogue just after the middle of the 18th century: straight wide roads and elegant "Parisian-style" mansions.

This is the most European district of Lisbon: the shops on the main thoroughfares (Rua Aurea, Rua Augusta, Rua da Prata) are some of the most exclusive in the city; the houses in the Baixa are the most sought-after and consequently the most expensive.

Other parts of the city conserve the memory of old Lisbon: the Bairro Alto, the ancient "journalists' quarter", which dominates the city from the top of a hill is linked to the Baixa by an unusual lift (Elevador do Carmo); the elegant and unfortunate Chiado, long a point of reference for the society and cultural life of Lisbon, greatly damaged by fire in 1988; Belém, home of the Tower of Belém, the Manueline Mosteiro dos Jerónimos – two of the most beautiful and prestigious buildings of Portuguese artistic history – and the brightly-coloured, narrow 17th-century houses of Rua Vieira Portuense; the castle of São Jorge, which closes the city to the rear, more garden and scenic spot than fortress.

Lisbon is rich in history and art and has turned its heritage to account: from the Museu Nacional de Arte Antiga, filled with records, some critical, of colonial imperialism (as is the case of the Japanese *namban*, which tell of the cruelty that accompanied the Portuguese conquests as seen through the eyes of those being colonised), to the Museu d'Agua Manuel de Maia (which records the difficult struggle against the problem of water shortage in the Portuguese capital), the Museu Nacional dos Coches, displaying some of the loveliest carriages of European aristocratic history, the Museu Nacional do Teatro, the Museu Nacional do Azulejo and the Museu da Marioneta. Unusual and disquieting is the Museu Arqueologico, set up in the ruins of the Igreja do Carmo. The church, built in the 14th century, is a ghostly reminder of the earthquake: its Gothic arcades, some of the few mediaeval parts that survived the tremor, support no vaults, and concerts are held in its roofless aisles in summer. It was never reconstructed because Lisbon wanted to remember that terrible day with an unconventional monument: nothing could be better suited than these haunting ruins.

Not all is historical in Lisbon but all is history. The capital has been, and wants to remain, the point of reference of that part of Portugal that still believes in great undertakings, as is demonstrated by three works completed this century. The Padrão dos Descobrimentos was commissioned in the years of the Salazar dictatorship, perhaps to boost its popularity. Today, with its row of heroes sculpted on the bow of a ship on the Tagus river, from Henry the Navigator to Vasco da Gama, it is an indication of the genuine bond between the peripheral post-colonial metropolis to that of the empire. The Padrao rises opposite the majestic statue of Cristo Rei and the 25 Abril bridge, the longest suspension bridge on the old continent. These were also strongly desired by Salazar; after the dictator's fall they became a symbol of rebirth: the former, with its great significance for humanity, links Lisbon ideally to Rio de Janeiro, the other Portuguese-speaking city to have its landscape dominated by Christ the Redeemer (and with which Portugal maintains excellent business relations); the latter reminiscent of the San Francisco Golden Gate, connects Lisbon with the south of the country but, most of all, lends a concrete form to the solid and proud spirit of the Portuguese people, dreamers capable of great works.

Every building of note, every flight of steps, every fountain and tower built after the 16th century bear the sometimes overbearing mark of the *azulejos*, omnipresent tiles peculiar to Portugal, as are Manueline style and the *fado*. In the noble dwellings of the 17th century the *azulejos* took the form of *tapetes* ("tapestries"), covering whole walls; in the 18th-century churches, the massive late-Baroque decorations are flanked by large panels depicting the lives

27 Azulejos, *an extraordinary example of unconventional art, are ceramic tiles painted to changing canons, styles and subjects, kiln-fired and widely applied in Portugal for decorative requirements. Some churches (such as the church of São Ildefonso at Oporto, shown here) exhibit* tapetes *("tapestries") of* azulejos *on religious themes in place of the traditional frescoes. The history of the* azulejos *reflects that of the country. Imported by the Arabs during their stay on Portuguese soil, they have over the centuries reflected in turn Italian, Flemish and even Afro-American tastes and manufacturing methods.*
The decorations and the use of colour are an indication of the culture that inspired them: blue and white with stylised and mainly geometrical designs were produced during the Moorish domination (the Koran prohibited the representation of human figures); polychrome and depicting courtly scenes – from hunting to love scenes – were made at times of major trading relations with northern Europe; religious subjects dominated during the years of the Counter-Reformation; and themes bound to seafaring conquests appeared at the height of colonialism.

28-29 *The monastery of Santa Maria da Vitória is a successful blend of Manueline, Renaissance and Gothic styles; its construction was started in 1385 at Batalha to celebrate the victory of the Portuguese over the Spanish at the battle of Aljubarrota. The sober and refined complex took over two hundred years to complete and boasts fine decorations in the ogives and along the portal. Of great beauty is the Claustro Real, or "royal cloister".*

30-31 *The internal courtyard of Mosteiro dos Jerónimos, in Lisbon, is perhaps the best-known example of Manueline style in Portugal. The wealth of decoration, mainly based on marine themes (a hawser motif is repeated along the entire length of the immense building), the precious materials and the majesty of the complex make the Mosteiro one of the major works of art in the country.*

32-33 *Praça Dom Pedro IV, known to the citizens of the capital as "the Rossio", is one of the cardinal points of Lisbon. Circular in shape, embellished with large fountains and surrounded by historical buildings of great value (including the unmistakable profile of the Teatro Nacional Dona Maria II) and numerous restaurants and bars, it is the point where the main city thoroughfares meet and is the hub of the Lisbon* movida.

of the saints painted on ceramics; at the street corners, even in the less elegant districts, the votive illustrations and street numbers are on brightly-coloured tiles. As for nearly all aspects of Portuguese life, the *azulejos* are the fruit of a coming together of different cultures: from the simple blue-white tiles of Arab origin to the more complex and coloured ceramics of Italian or Flemish inspiration, from the geometrical oriental-style decorations to religious or aristocratic subjects.
The reflection of long centuries of Portuguese history, *azulejos* are more common on the coast, especially in Lisbon, than inland. The reason is clear: the sea ports experienced ethnic influxes of all types, from the Arab invasions to the "rebound" migrations from the colonies. Here the different flairs, a bit African, a bit Latin-American, a bit European, are concentrated and blend to raise these ceramic squares from mere tiles to works of art. And it is here, on the Atlantic coast but above all in the capital, that the ethnic differences produce the most unusual cultural and racial mixes: dark skin and green eyes, African bodies and Mediterranean features.

Portugal has a thousand faces but just one soul. For those not born within the narrow Portuguese boundaries, its soul may be the melody heard in the small bars, in Lisbon as in Coimbra too, sung by a *fadista* and played on two guitars. This is the *fado*, popular Portuguese music, a melancholic song perhaps taken from the troubadours of Provence, perhaps from Brazil or Africa: a cultural undertow, another rebound of the colonial heritage, that materialises to great effect in the *saudade*, impossible to translate but which means "indulging languidly in nostalgia". This mood is peculiar to the Portuguese, even the most dynamic.

Portugal is a strange country, a land of bold enterprise and passive abandonment, of monotony and originality, of wealth and poverty, but never ordinary: not even in the most "touristy" areas such as the Algarve, a coast of rare beauty with a flattering and well-deserved name (*al-Gharb*, in Arabic "garden of the west"). This area is an Afro-Mediterranean garden where olive groves, orange and lemon trees stand alongside carob, almond and fig trees; the climate, warm and temperate thanks to the mountains that protect the Algarve from the cold winds of the north, has made it a bathers' paradise. The coasts, flat and sandy to the west, rugged and broken by tiny beaches farther south, are the new promised land for hundreds of thousands of tourists seeking an untamed territory. A little building speculation, inevitable wherever there is money – especially if foreign – has not yet changed the face of the region that housed the general headquarters of Henry the Navigator.

In Portugal some swear that the new challenge to the world will start from here again, as in the 15th century; but not with galleons and caravels. The heroes of the year two thousand will control bathing establishments, museums, tourist itineraries. From conquerors to conquered, the Portuguese will find gold and riches at home, by promoting and exploiting, at last, the exceptional natural and historical riches of a land that was once on the edge of the world.

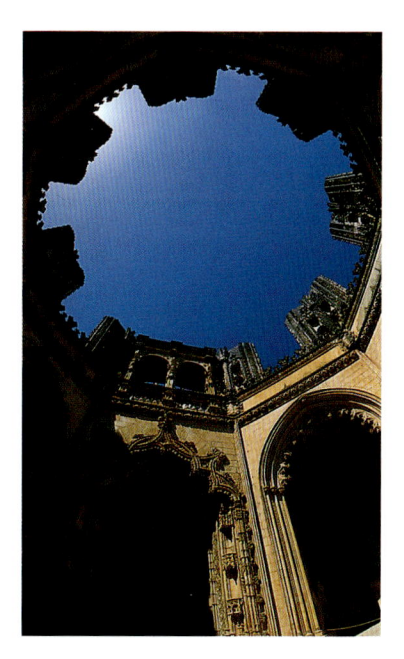

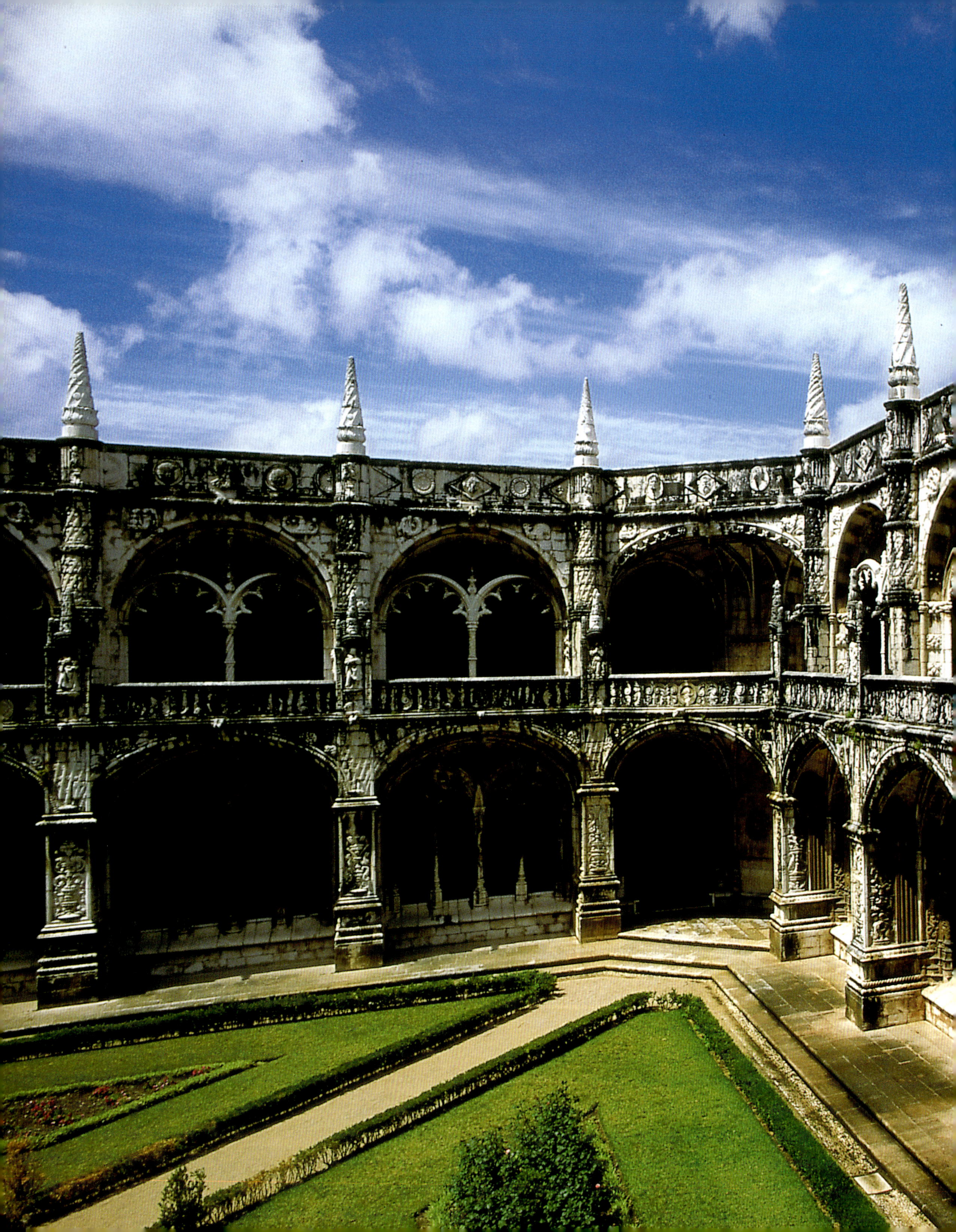

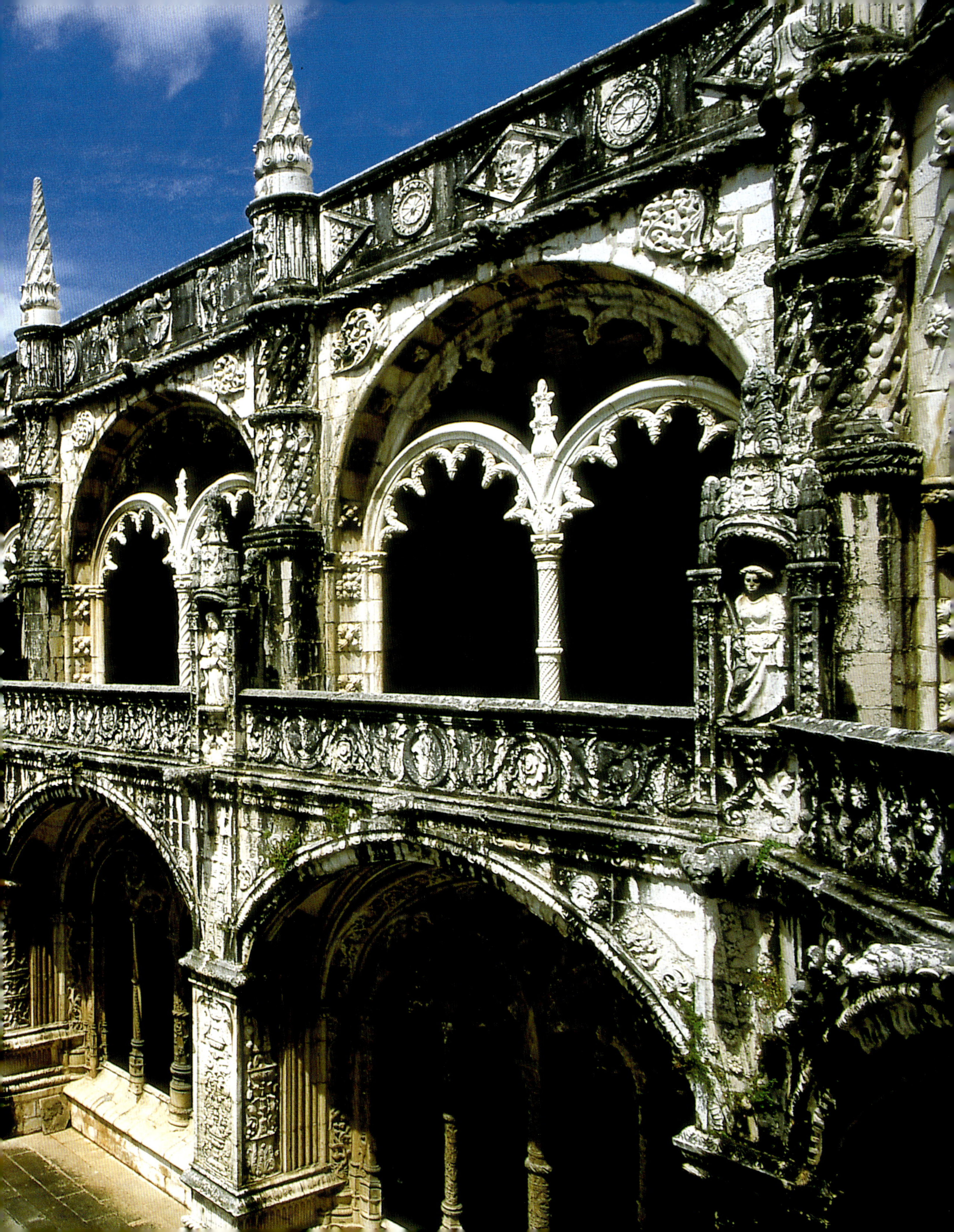

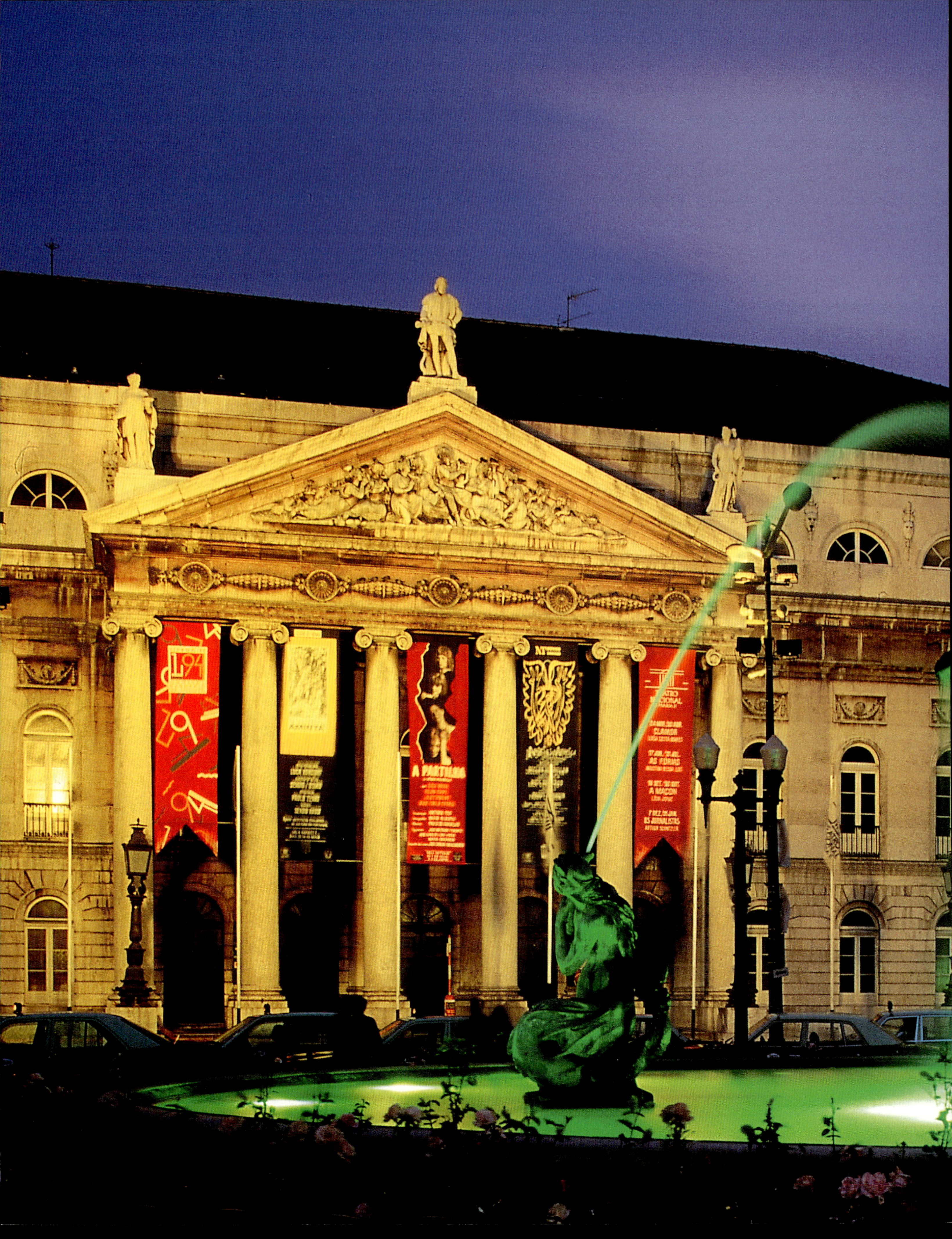
A PARTILHA
CLAMOR
AS FÚRIAS
A MAÇON
OS JORNALISTAS

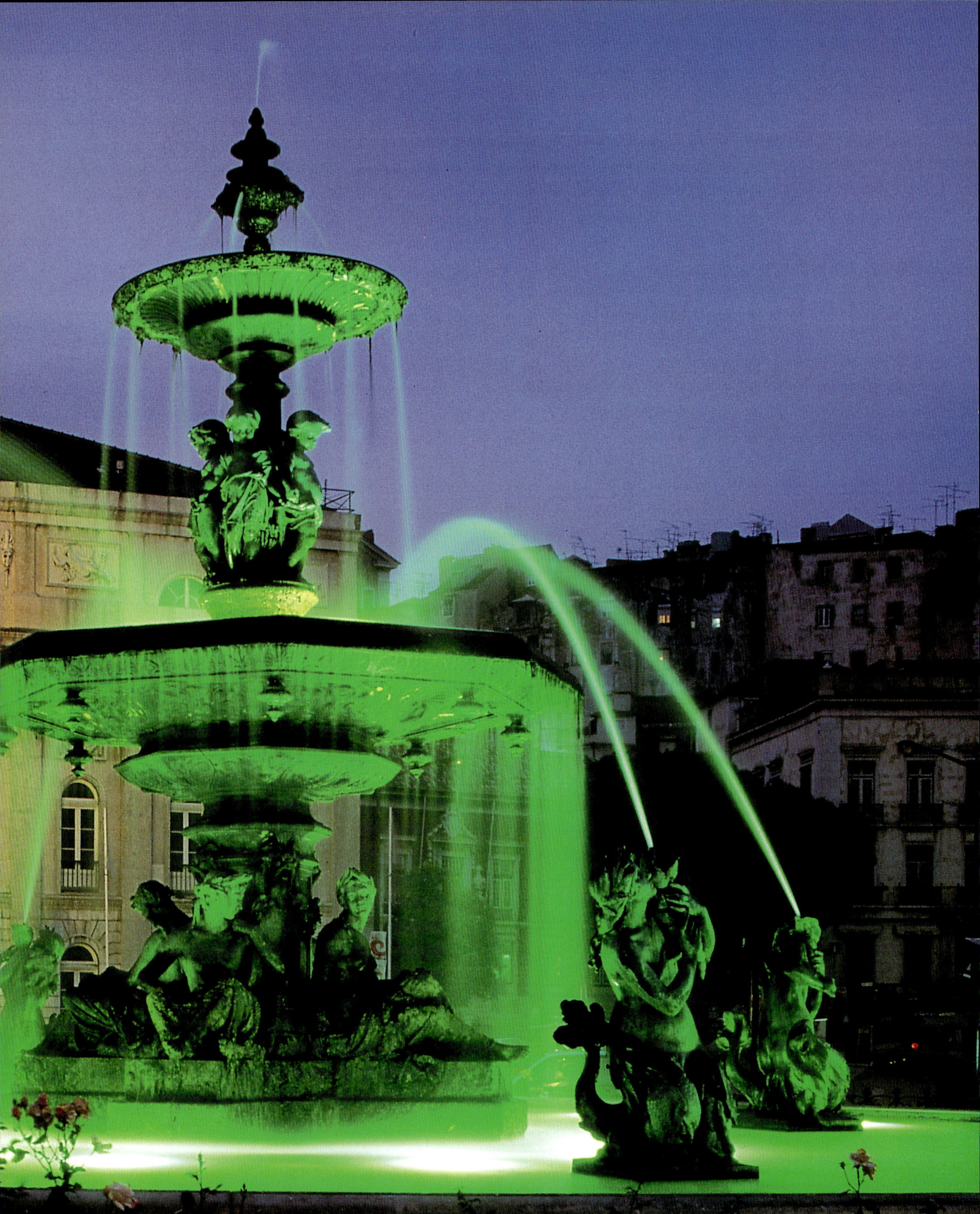

Rolling hills and golden sands

34 top The island of Corvo is the smallest of the western Azores. Vila Nova de Corvo, the tiny town seen in the picture (the island of Flores is visible in the distance), has no more than 400 permanent inhabitants.

34 bottom The territory commonly known as the Minho covers a larger area than that traced by the small, lush Rio Minho valley, in the extreme north of Portugal. In the valleys formed by the Lima, Cávado, Homem and Tamega rivers the scenery is an alternation of terraced farmland (usually vines) and wild reliefs, with a sprinkling of chestnut trees.

35 The Minho offers extremely beautiful views. Plentiful in water, closed to the north by the mountains of Spanish Galicia and to the east by the serras of Trás-os-Montes, it is a region of extremes: dark sheets of water, pine and chestnut trees, small villages perched on the mountains or squashed at the bottom of the valley and verdant scenery all around.

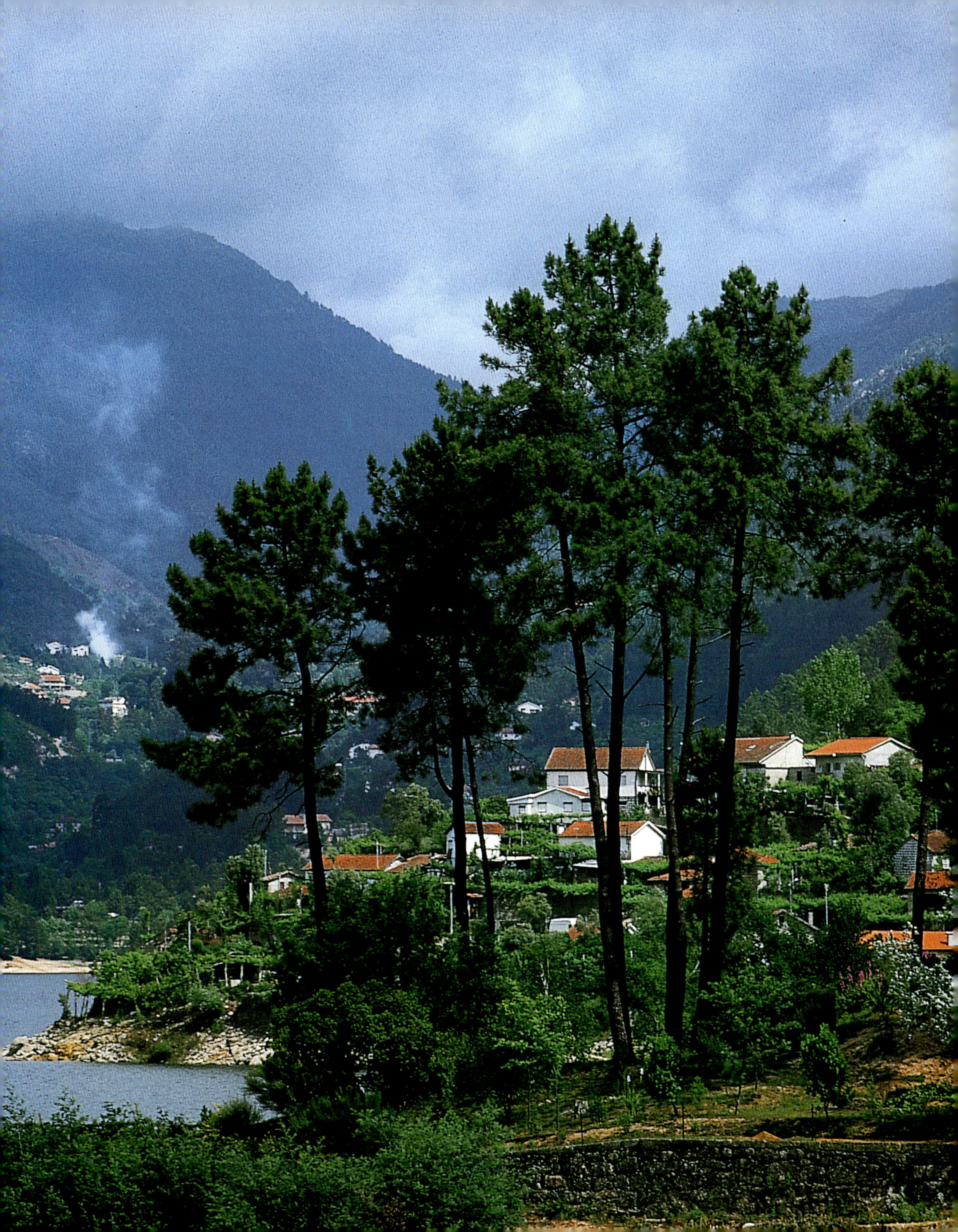

The Minho, the green heart of Portugal

36 top and centre *The whole Minho region, watered by the intense rainfall typical of the oceanic climate of northern Portugal, abounds in water; this is trapped in unusual artificial lakes called* barragems. *Small villages, prized crops and wild vegetation sit on the shores of these basins.*

36 bottom *The rainfall is limited to eight months of the year and gives way to a period of relative dryness during the summer months. Thanks to this climate the Minho valleys contain areas of intensive vine cultivation, which represents one of the region's few resources.*

36-37 *The Serra de Gerês is part of the Peneda-Gerês National Park, a magnificent nature reserve north-east of Braga, in the Minho. It is reached from Viana do Castelo, along the road that leads to the* barragems. *Natural and historic beauties mingle in the heart of the park – the Baroque palaces of Ponte de Lima, Romanesque bridges, paths in the forests, spectacular views of the surrounding mountains and dams that supply the whole region with electricity.*

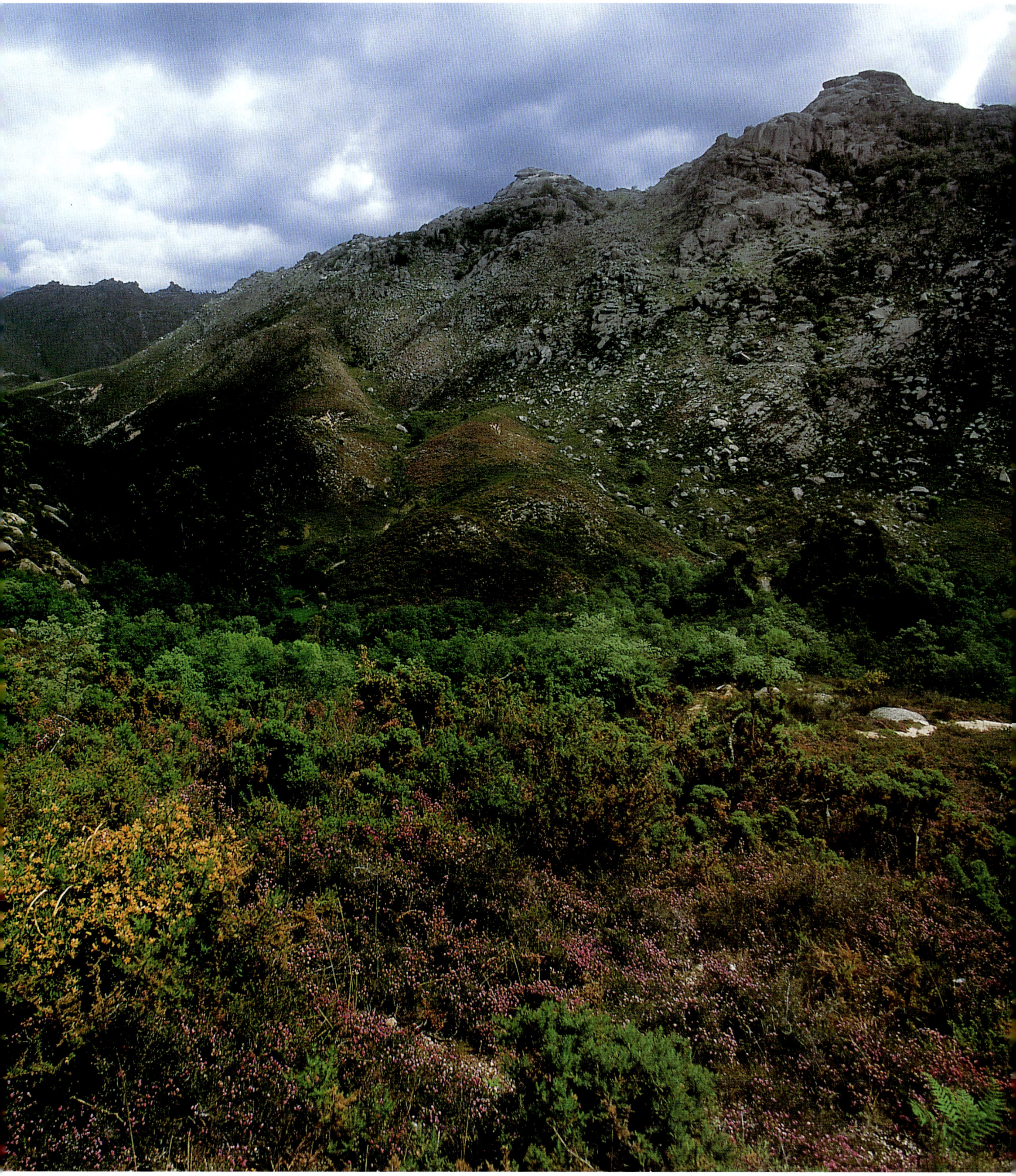

Looking out on the Atlantic

38 *Azenhas do Mar: the ocean heaves against the rocks and sheer above the sea stand the fishermen's houses; 160 feet below, bathers splash in a hotel swimming pool. This too is Portugal: the work of man constantly contrasted with a fantastic, untamed nature.*

39 top *Beaten by strong winds all year round and situated approximately 460 feet above sea level, Cabo da Roca is the westernmost point of Portugal. It is wrongly believed to be one of the extremes of Europe, but the coasts of both Iceland and Ireland lie farther west.*

39 bottom *An extension of the Serra da Sintra, Cabo da Roca has, in the popular imagination, taken over from Cabo São Vicente, on the Algarve, long thought to be "the extreme edge of the world". The unceasing action of the ocean, shown here in all its might, has eroded the rock, creating a jagged coast full of delightfully secluded spots.*

Wine-producing country

40-41 The Rio Douro valley (literally "river of gold") is one of the most fascinating regions in Portugal. Here they harvest some of the world's most famous grapes; the peasants have terraced the sides of the high ground and during the harvest the men shoulder funnel-shaped baskets weighing more than 70 kilograms. Two of the wines produced with these grapes are very famous: vinho verde *takes its name from the colour of the grapes and is a light wine;* vinho porto *is aged for between three and forty years and has a full bodied flavour and a sturdy soul. The latter wine has been the object of commerce for more than three hundred years, when a peace treaty established free trading between England and Portugal. Legend tells that two English merchants invented port as it is known today by pouring strong liquor into the wine to stabilise it during transportation. What is not legend is that some of the largest cellars were founded by the English between the 17th and 18th centuries.*

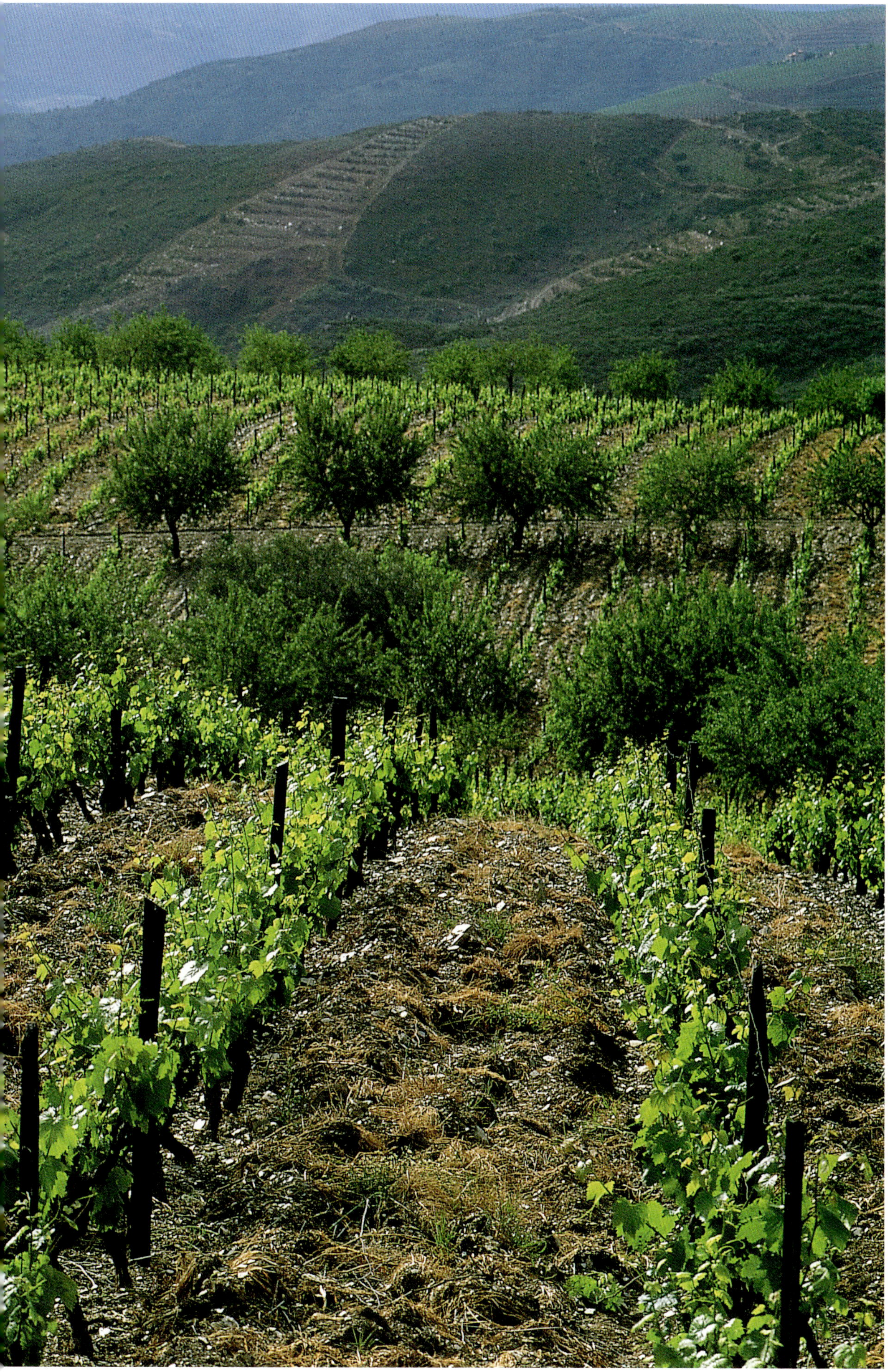

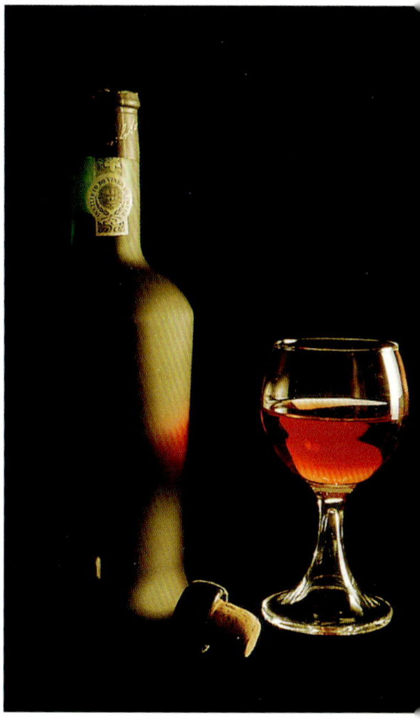

Sun-drenched coasts

42-43 Some postcards of Nazaré still show the fishermen, berets on their heads, drawing the boats out of the water aided by a pair of oxen. This tradition survived until just a few years ago on what many, quite rightly, consider the most authentic Portuguese coastline. The Algarve may be a gift of nature – sea and tropical sands – but the Costa da Prata, especially in the immediate vicinity of Nazaré, is the Portugal of the ocean, rich and poor at the same time, fascinating and untamed despite the passing years and a never-ending stream of tourists. The Nazaré beach has been immortalised by generations of painters and photographers: fishermen busy mending nets, brightly-decorated boats drawn up, fish left to dry in the sun, the sometimes violent sometime gentle waves of the Atlantic and small houses huddled together on the coast.

In summer, when the weather is good, it looks like the Mediterranean and is popular with surfers and wind-surfers; in winter, or in bad weather, the sea becomes master, eating up wide strips of sand and hiding the houses in thick fog. The village of Sitio peeks out from the top of a large rocky spur that shelters the village and keeps the strong wind that normally lashes the coast away from the beach.

43

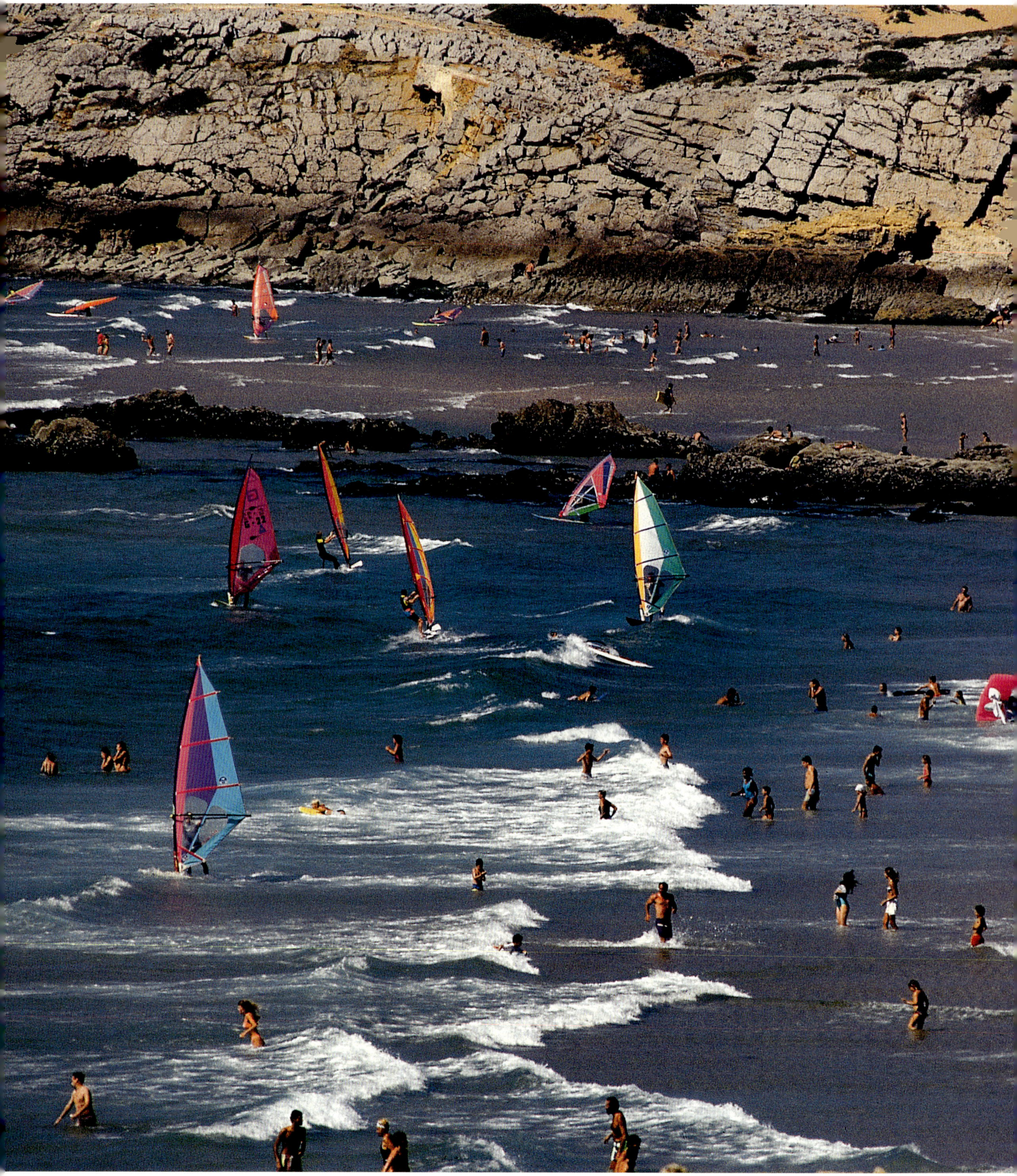

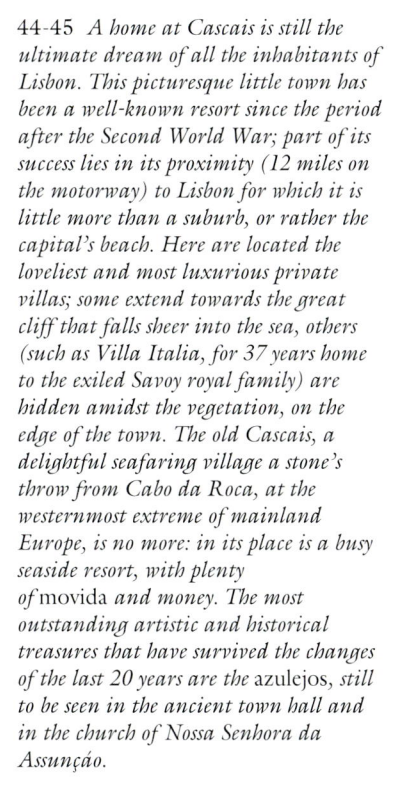

44-45 *A home at Cascais is still the ultimate dream of all the inhabitants of Lisbon. This picturesque little town has been a well-known resort since the period after the Second World War; part of its success lies in its proximity (12 miles on the motorway) to Lisbon for which it is little more than a suburb, or rather the capital's beach. Here are located the loveliest and most luxurious private villas; some extend towards the great cliff that falls sheer into the sea, others (such as Villa Italia, for 37 years home to the exiled Savoy royal family) are hidden amidst the vegetation, on the edge of the town. The old Cascais, a delightful seafaring village a stone's throw from Cabo da Roca, at the westernmost extreme of mainland Europe, is no more: in its place is a busy seaside resort, with plenty of* movida *and money. The most outstanding artistic and historical treasures that have survived the changes of the last 20 years are the* azulejos, *still to be seen in the ancient town hall and in the church of Nossa Senhora da Assunção.*

Alentejo, the granary of the country

46 left Monsarez is an ancient village-fortress on the border between the Alentejo and Spain which has maintained the original traits of the mediaeval village.

46 right Estremoz stands at the centre of that vast semi-level region called Alentejo, situated east of Lisbon. It owes its fortune to the memorable azulejo factory and the presence of one of the numerous royal country residences, now converted into a pousada *(guest-house).*

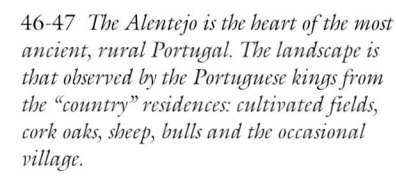

46-47 The Alentejo is the heart of the most ancient, rural Portugal. The landscape is that observed by the Portuguese kings from the "country" residences: cultivated fields, cork oaks, sheep, bulls and the occasional village.

48-49 The Alentejo is patronised by a high-class, sentimental and nostalgic tourism; the Braganzas spent much time here and this is where some of the most resolute democratic petitions originated. The most attractive local residences have been turned into pousadas *to accommodate this "sentimental" tourism.*

50-51 The picturesque village of Monsanto in Beira was, in the Fifties, declared "the most characteristic village in Portugal". The granite dwellings, flower-lined streets and the light Manueline decorations won it a silver cockerel award, which is still perched on the church bell-tower.

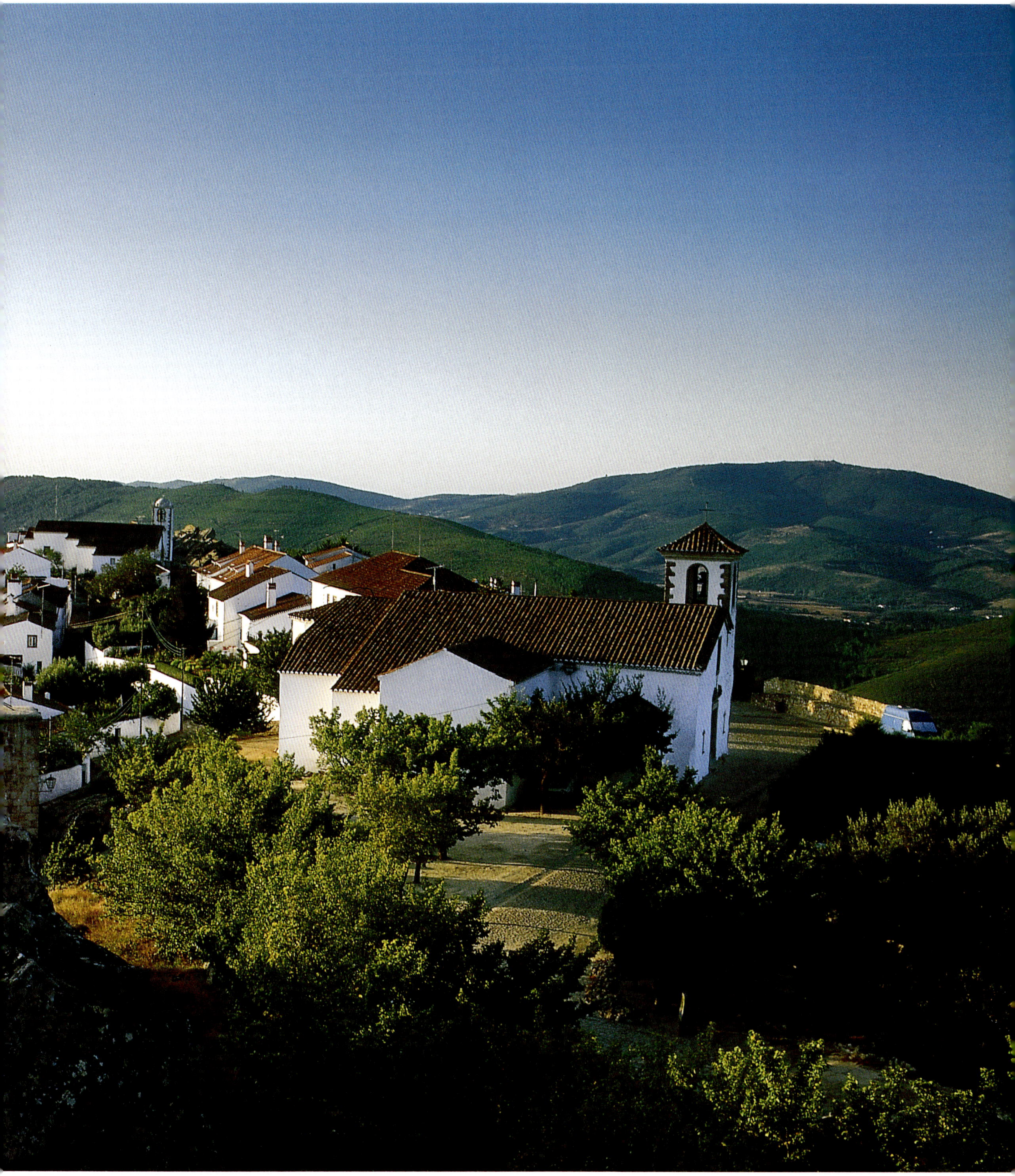

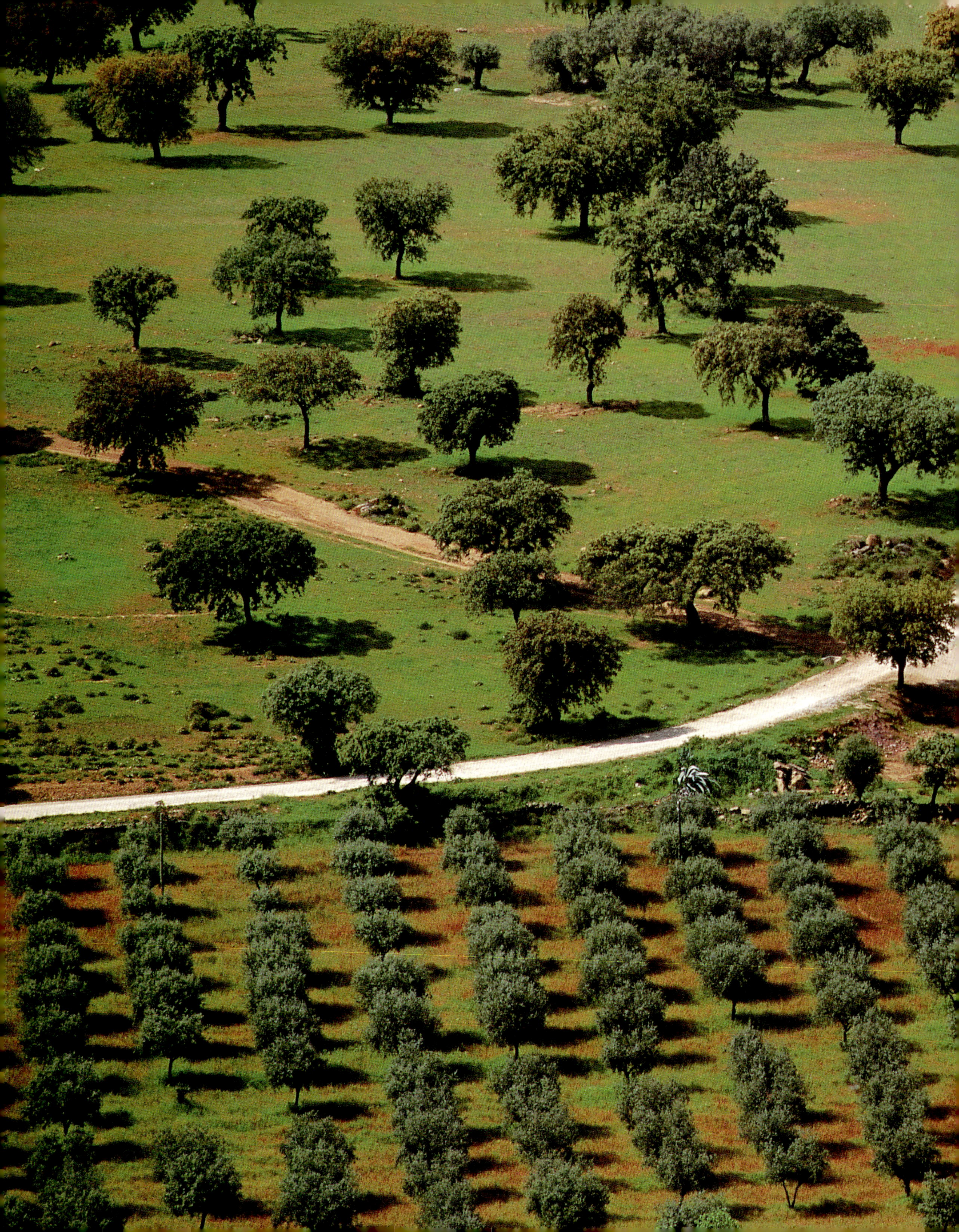

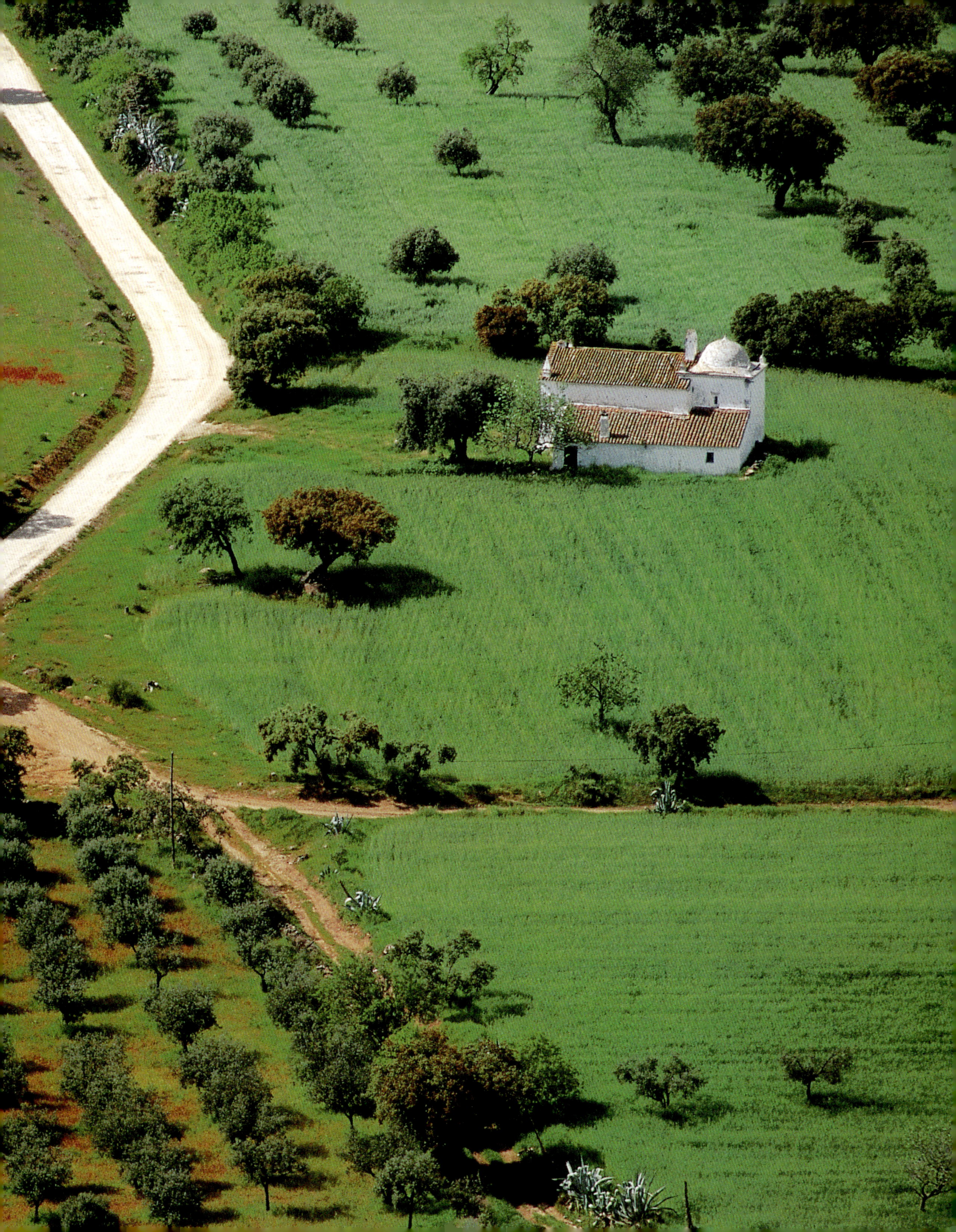

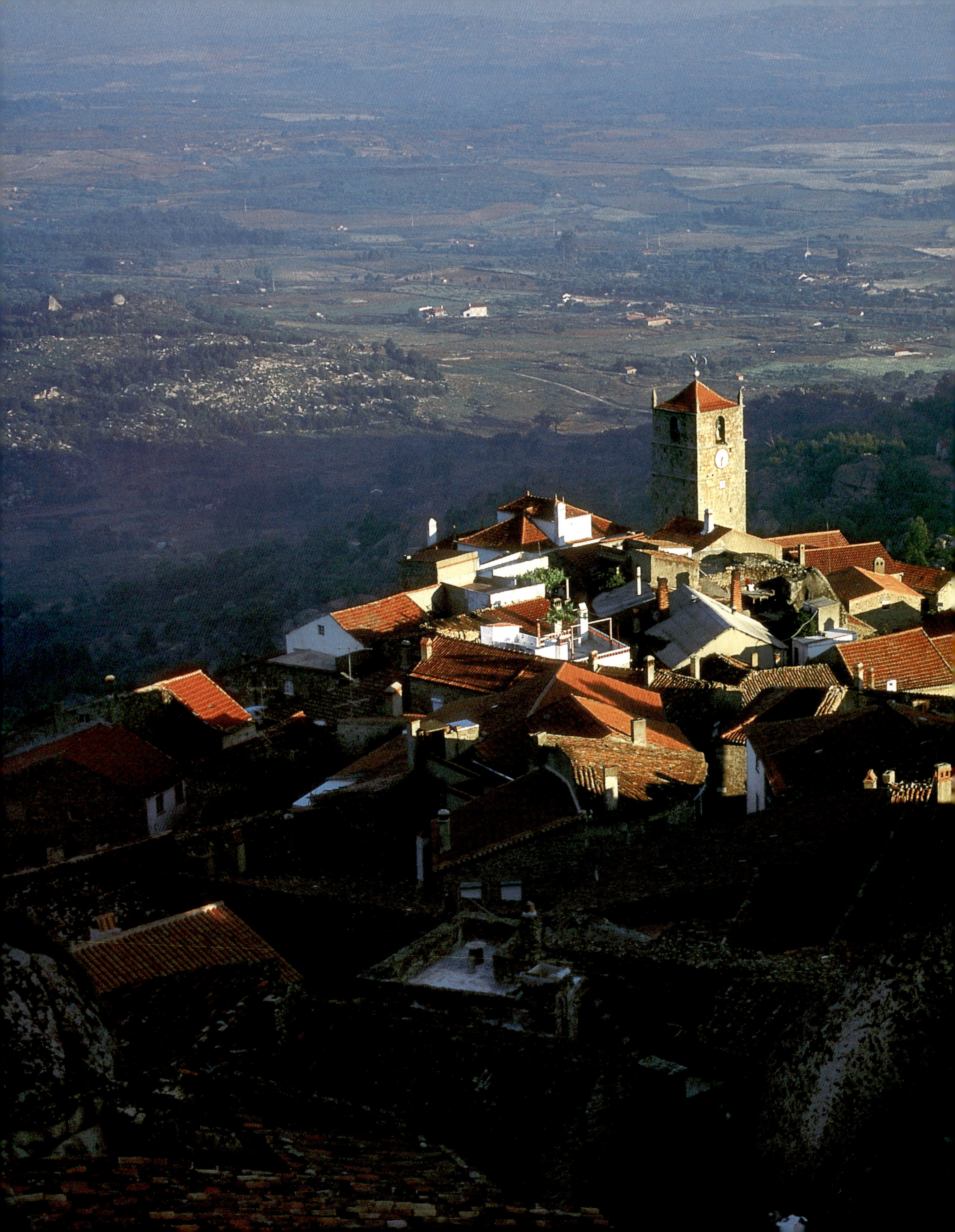

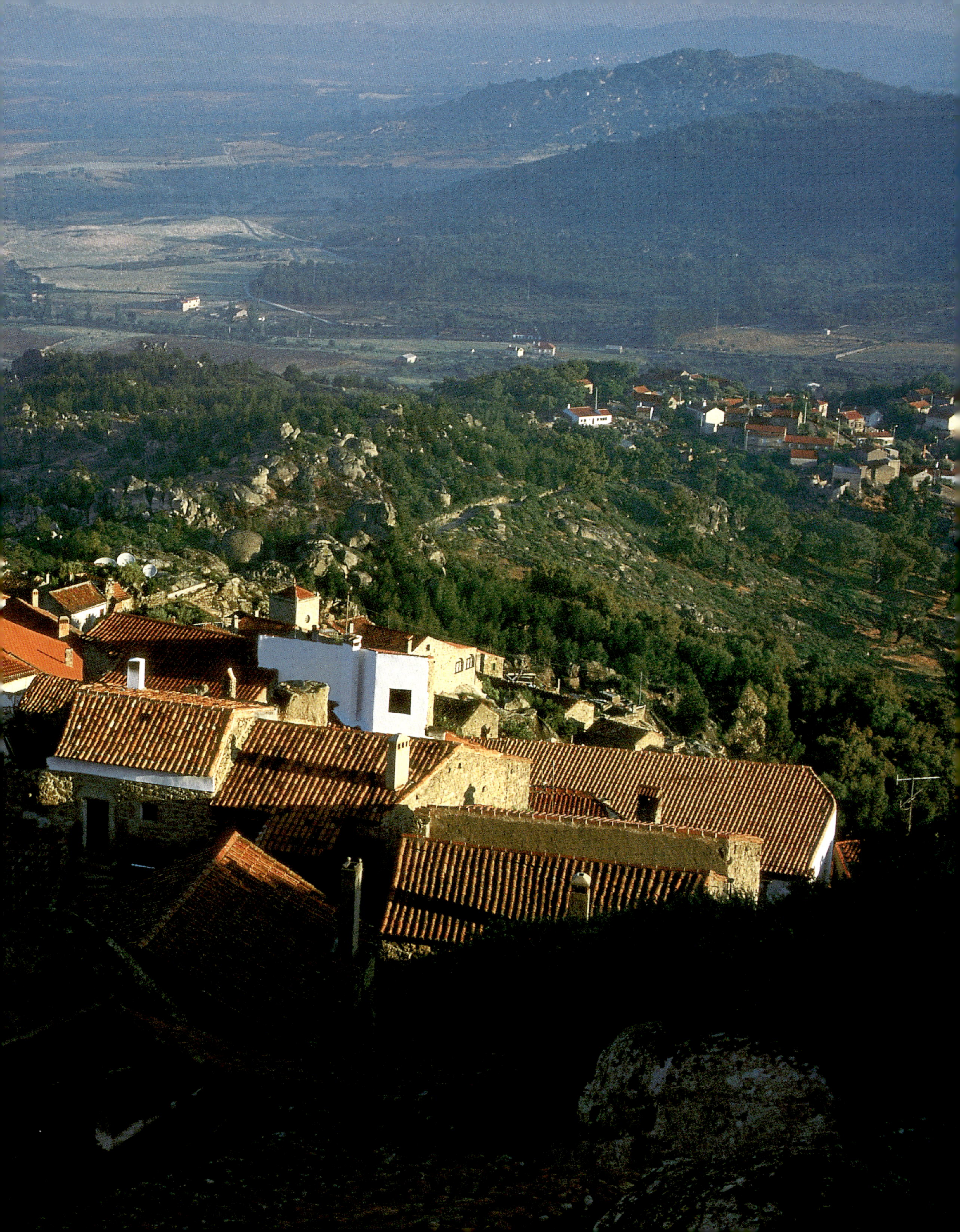

The Algarve, the garden of the west

52 top *Long considered the edge of the world, Cabo São Vicente is the westernmost tip of the Algarve.*

52 bottom *The extraordinary morphology of the Algarve (from the Arabic al-Gharb "garden of the west") offers fantastic views; in some parts (as seen in the photograph at Sagres) the coast is cut into cliffs forming small inlets with delightful beaches; farther east the coast is flat with huge beaches and coastal lagoons closed to the rear by great dunes.*

53 top   Midway between Portimão and Lagos, Praia da Rocha is one of the most famous spots on the Algarve. In the early 20th century, Praia da Rocha was already renowned for its fine sandy beaches, backed by erratically-shaped rocks eroded by the sea and for its crystal-clear waters.

53 bottom   The coast of Portimão, a well-known tourist resort in the heart of the Algarve, affords splendid views and is a paradise for sea dogs; the sheer rocks form small bays in which to anchor, sheltered from the winds. Portimão has a memorable marine tradition; it is the most important port in the region and its inhabitants still make a living from tourism and sardine fishing.

54-55   White houses protruding towards the sea, the characteristic coloured boats of the fishermen, a clear blue sky all year round: the village of Ferragudo is all the beauty of the Algarve in a nutshell.

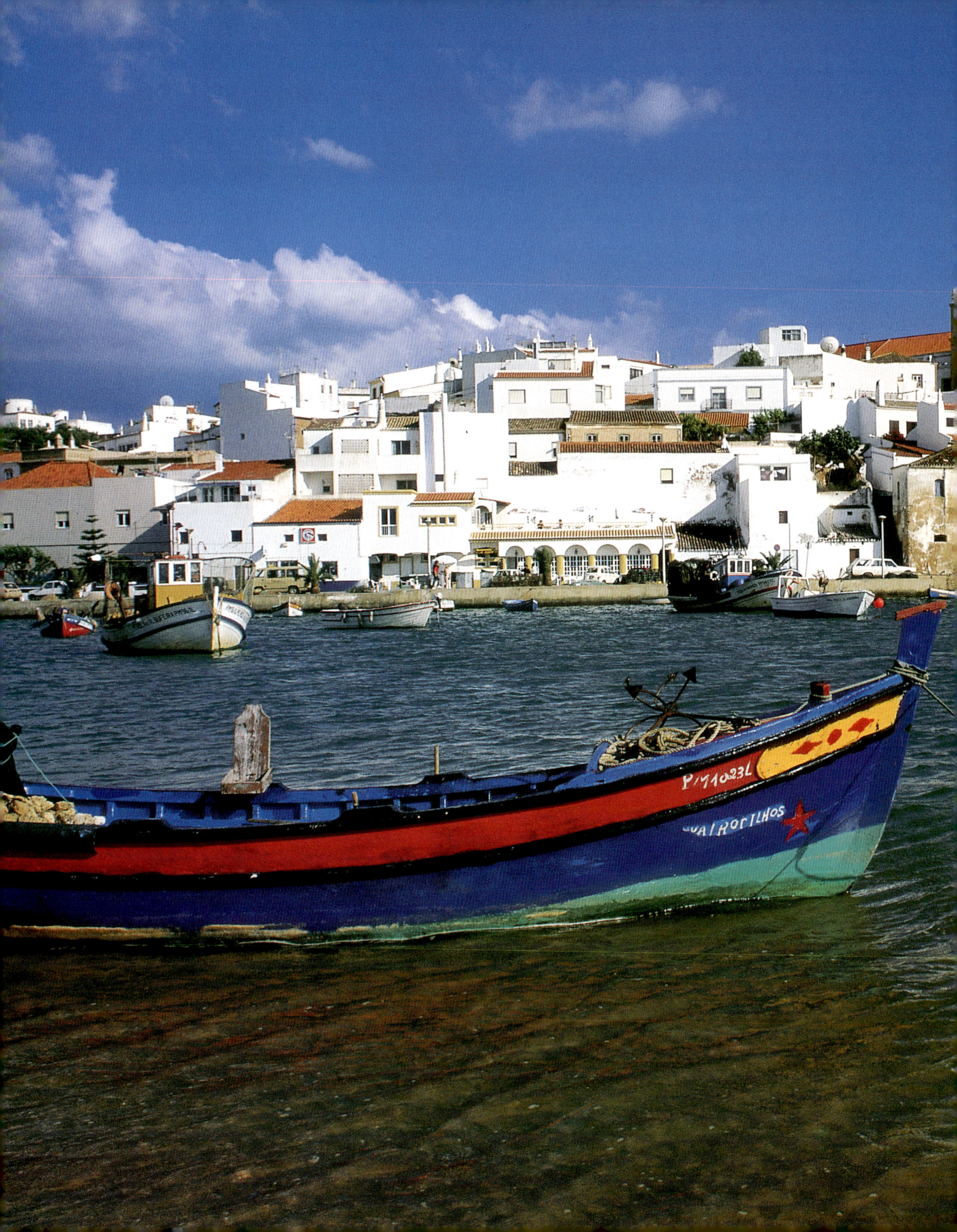

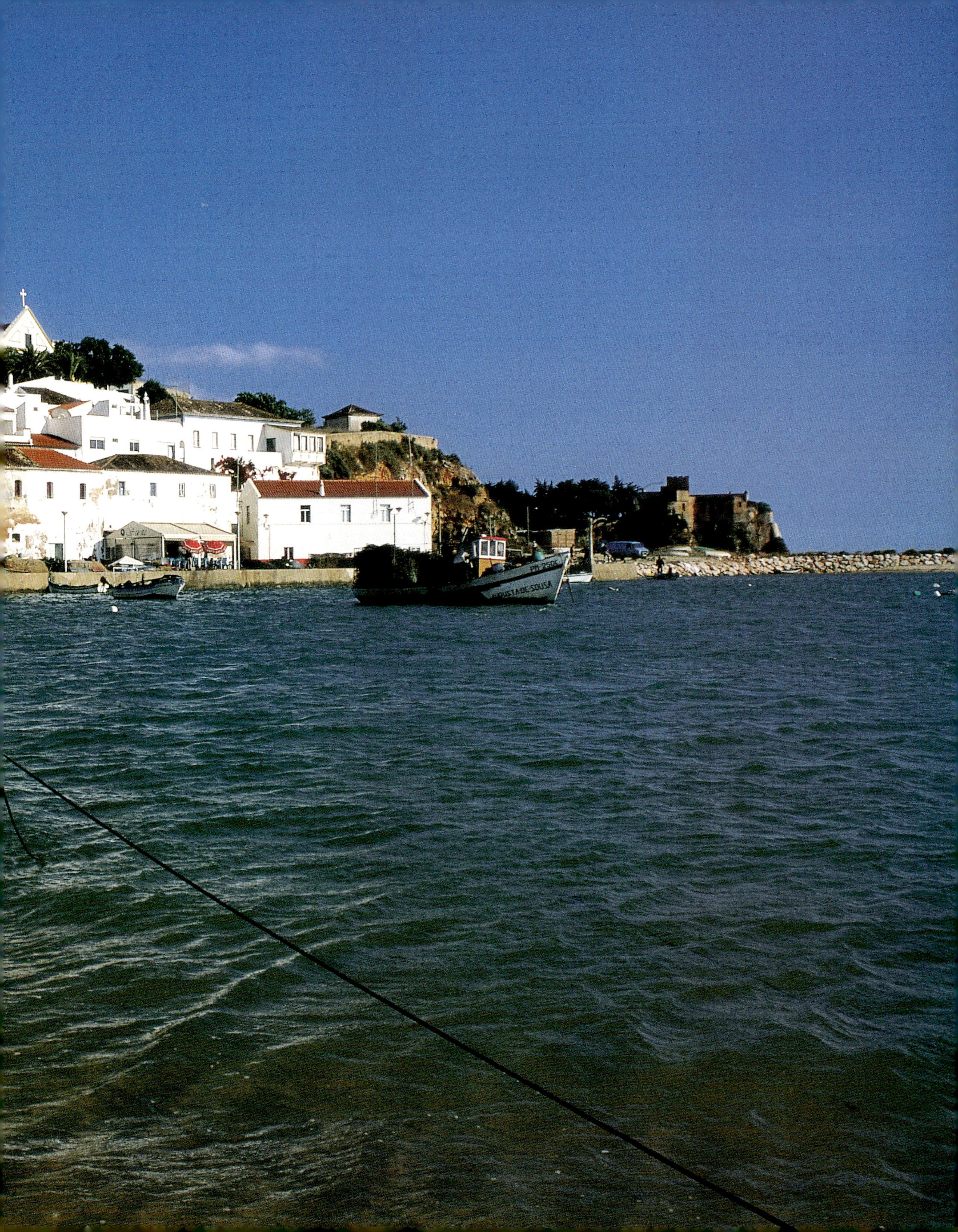

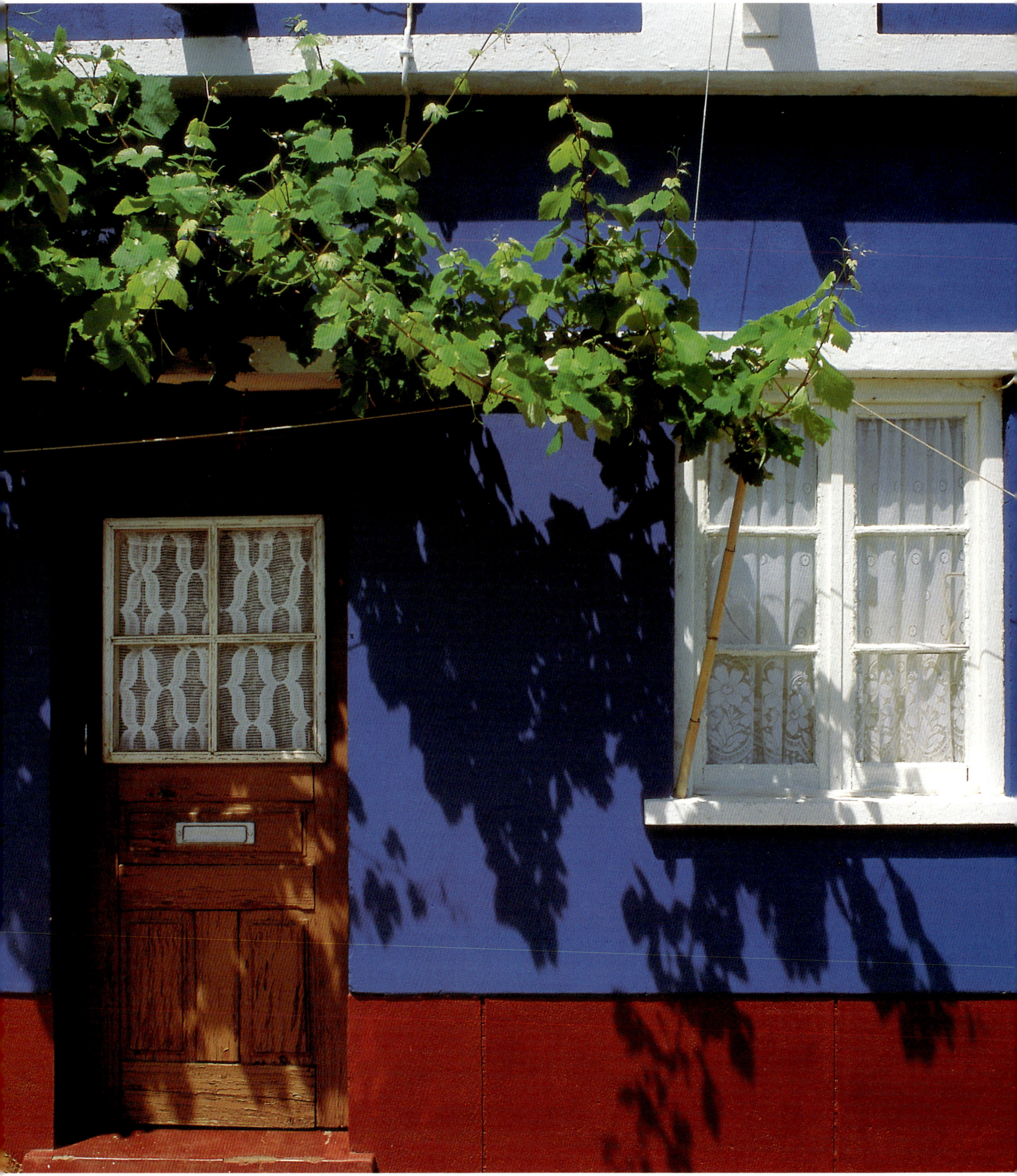

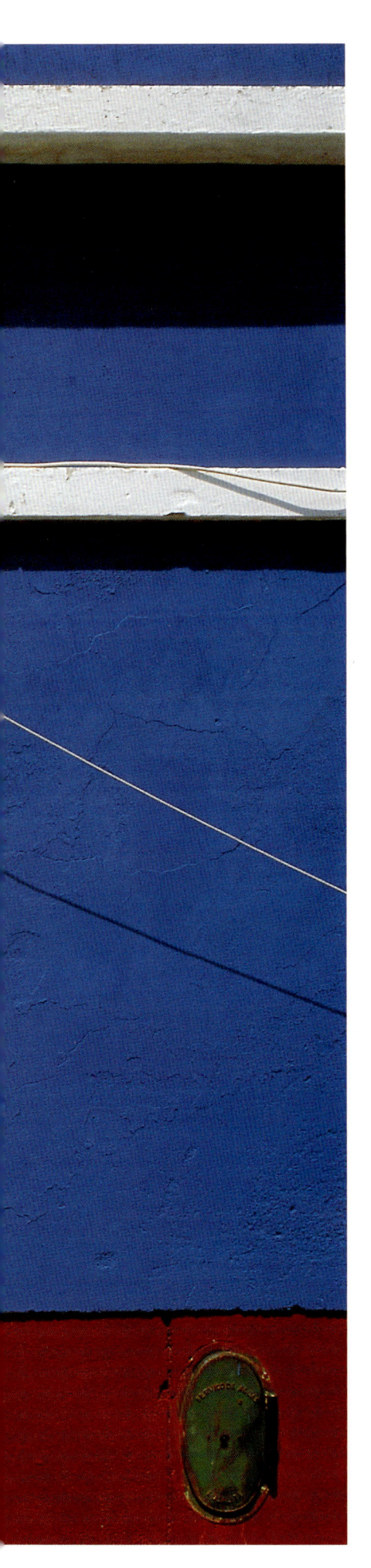

56-57 Colour is a fundamental component on the Portuguese landscape: white walls and blue decorations are reminiscent of typically Mediterranean traditions; the red and green much used on boats are the favourite colours of the Portuguese people and appear on the national flag. For this house at Vila di Bispo on the Algarve the traditional colours have been inverted: deep blue (with a touch of red) on the outside walls and white stucco-work and shutters.

57 top and centre Vila do Bispo is a pretty seaside village situated 6 miles north of Sagres. Despite the tourist boom of recent years, the village has conserved its original appearance with small, blue and white houses, narrow streets, azulejos and India rubber trees used for decoration.

57 bottom Tavira is a small town on the Algarve a few miles from Spain; it is famous for its 17th-century bridge over the Rio Assêca, for the Moorish castle that dominates the town and for its past importance as a port. During its long history, the life of Tavira has always been inseparably bound to the sea and this is manifest in the decorations embellishing the churches; both inside and out, as the picture shows, there is a prevalence of marine motifs (shells, stylised figure-heads, waves, sea horses).

58-59 The most impressive rock of the Algarve (more than 500 feet high) rises from the sea near Vila do Bispo. All along the coast small, golden beaches give way to rocky stretches, eroded for centuries by the sea to form underground passages which fill with roaring waves.

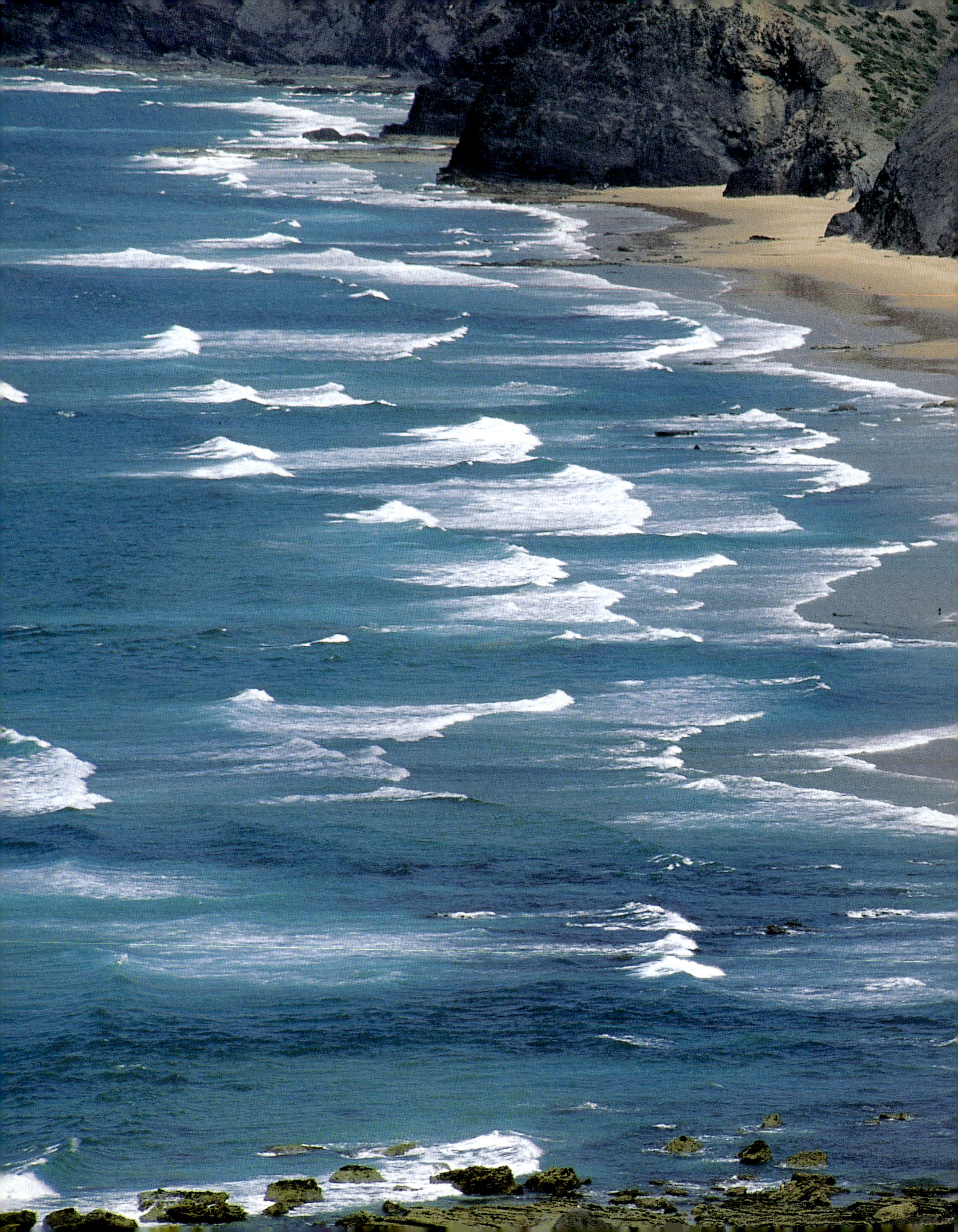

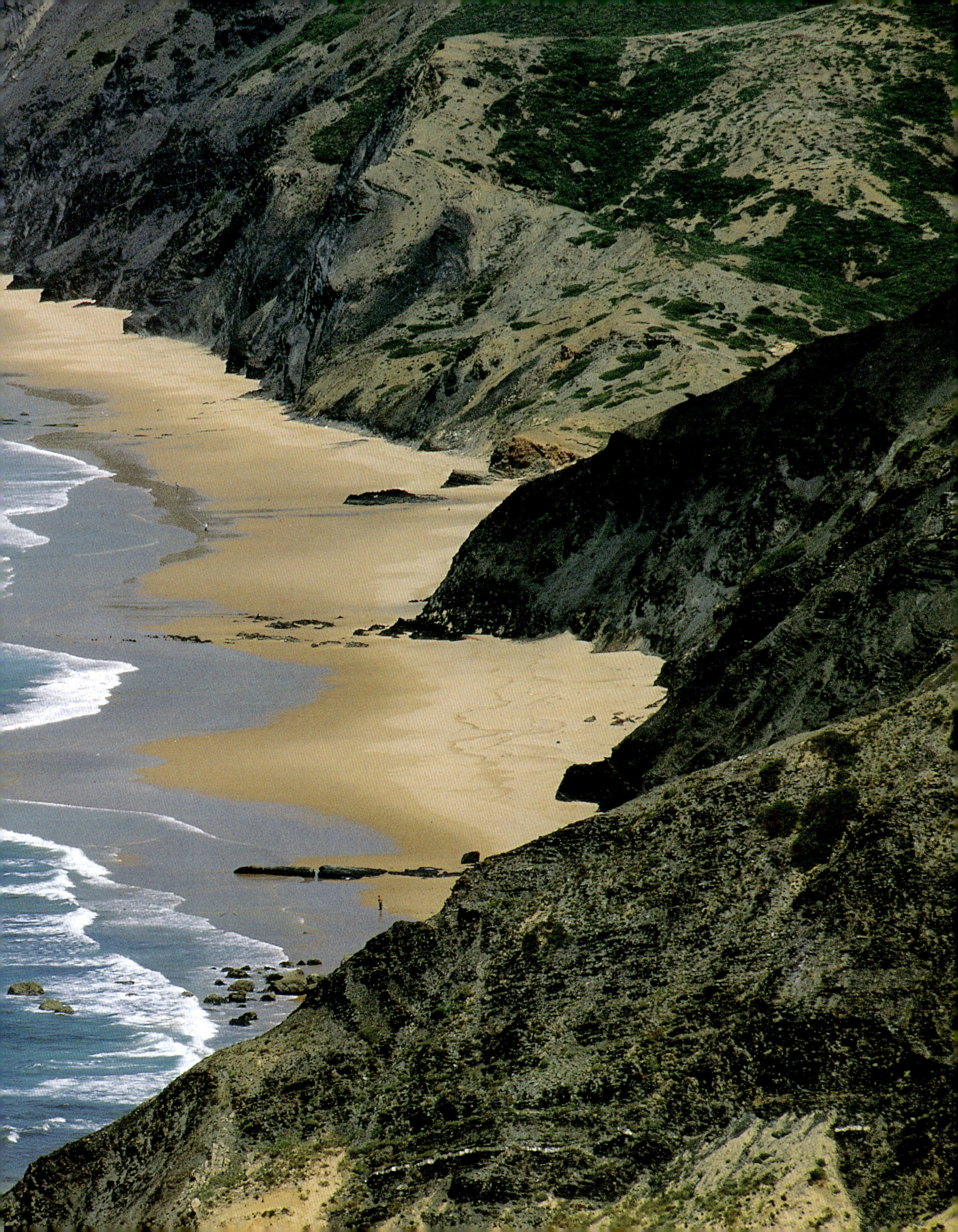

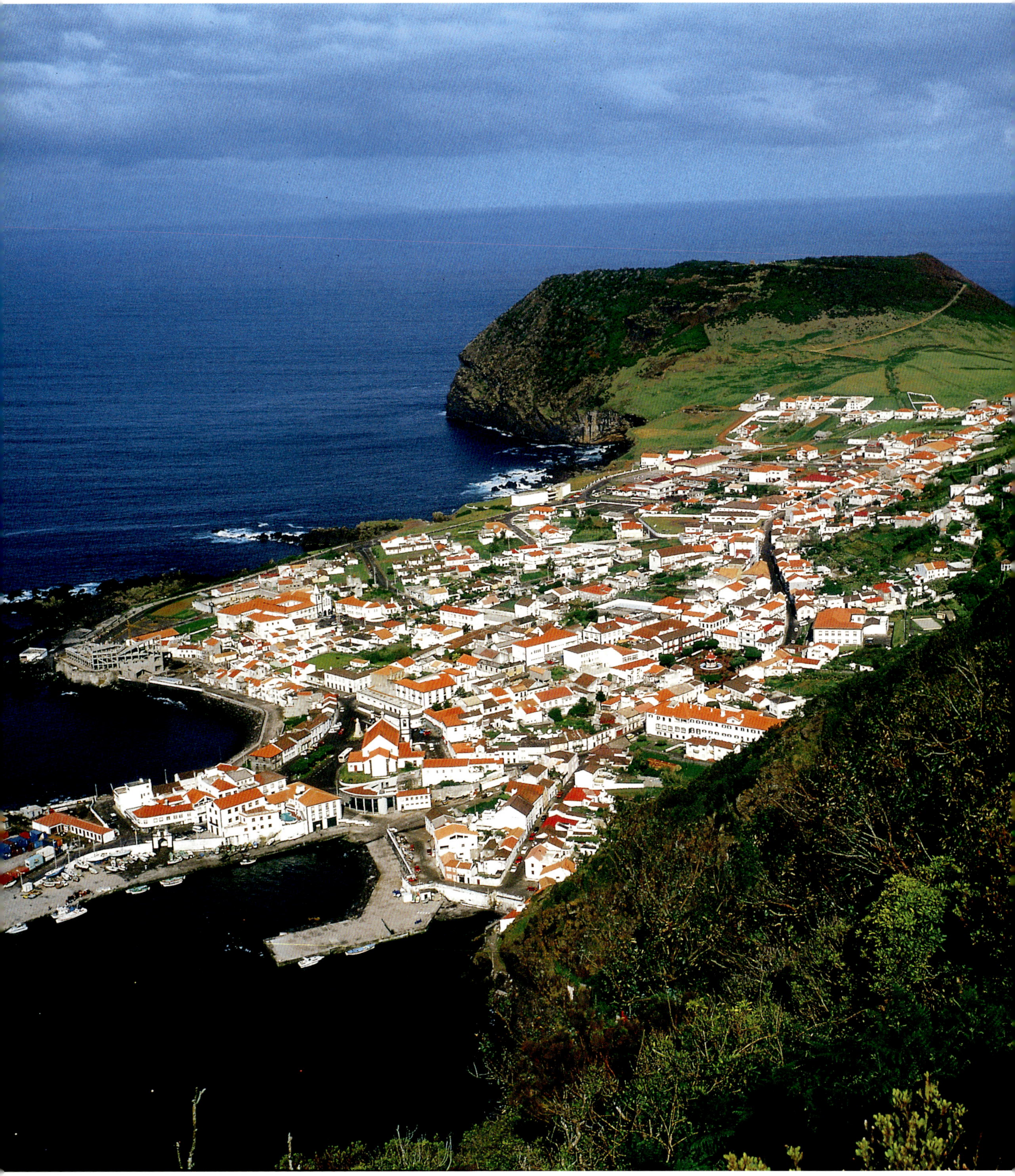

Madeira and the Azores, the islands of flowers

60-61 The port of Velas is the largest town of São Jorge, in the Azores. Lying in the heart of the archipelago, the island is mainly mountainous (with one peak rising to 3,494 feet) and rich in lush vegetation.

61 left A photograph taken beneath the Flamengos mill is a must for tourists passing through Fayal, one of the smallest islands of the archipelago of the Azores. The island was named after the Myrica faya tree commonly found on the island.

61 top right For its size and beauty, São Miguel is the most famous of the Azores; it is of volcanic origin as clearly seen in this picture of one of the island's lagoons, formed by thousands of years of eruptions.

61 bottom right Teeming with flowers and not at all wild, despite having maintained its original appearance, blessed by a climate mild all year round and steady winds, the Azores are a paradise for sailing and deep-sea fishing enthusiasts. Together with Fayas, Pico (the island in the photograph) houses the Museu dos Baleeiros, dedicated to marine traditions and filled with exhibits relating to the whale-hunting practised here in ancient times. Pico owes its name to the mountain that dominates the landscape, an extinct volcano, at 7,609 feet the highest peak in the Azores.

62 top Angra – its full name is Angra do Heroismo – is the only inhabited town on Terceira and the most important town in the Azores. An unadulterated example of a Renaissance village, it has been declared a world heritage site by UNESCO.

62 centre The island of Terceira was, for centuries, an obligatory stop for ships about to sail round Africa and head for India. All the major expeditions of the great Portuguese navigators, from Diaz to Da Gama stopped here for supplies or to shelter from the storms. The highest point on the island and long a landmark for navigators is the Caldera de Santa Barbara.

62 bottom Terceira is famous the world over for its bullfights which differ from those of both Spain (bloodier) and those of Portugal (highly ritual and less bloody). As the name tourada da corda suggests, the bull is dragged through the streets tied to a rope. Naturally the bull frees itself quite easily from this inadequate "leash" and runs free through the crowd, provoked by the most valiant who try to regain control.

62-63 Although it is the local craftsmanship – objects made by working fig tree pith or fish scales – that has made it famous all over the world, Flores, the most westerly of the Azores, boasts natural beauties that make it unique. It has an extremely uneven terrain, waterfalls, numerous volcanic lakes and thick vegetation dominated by brightly-coloured fragrant tropical flowers.

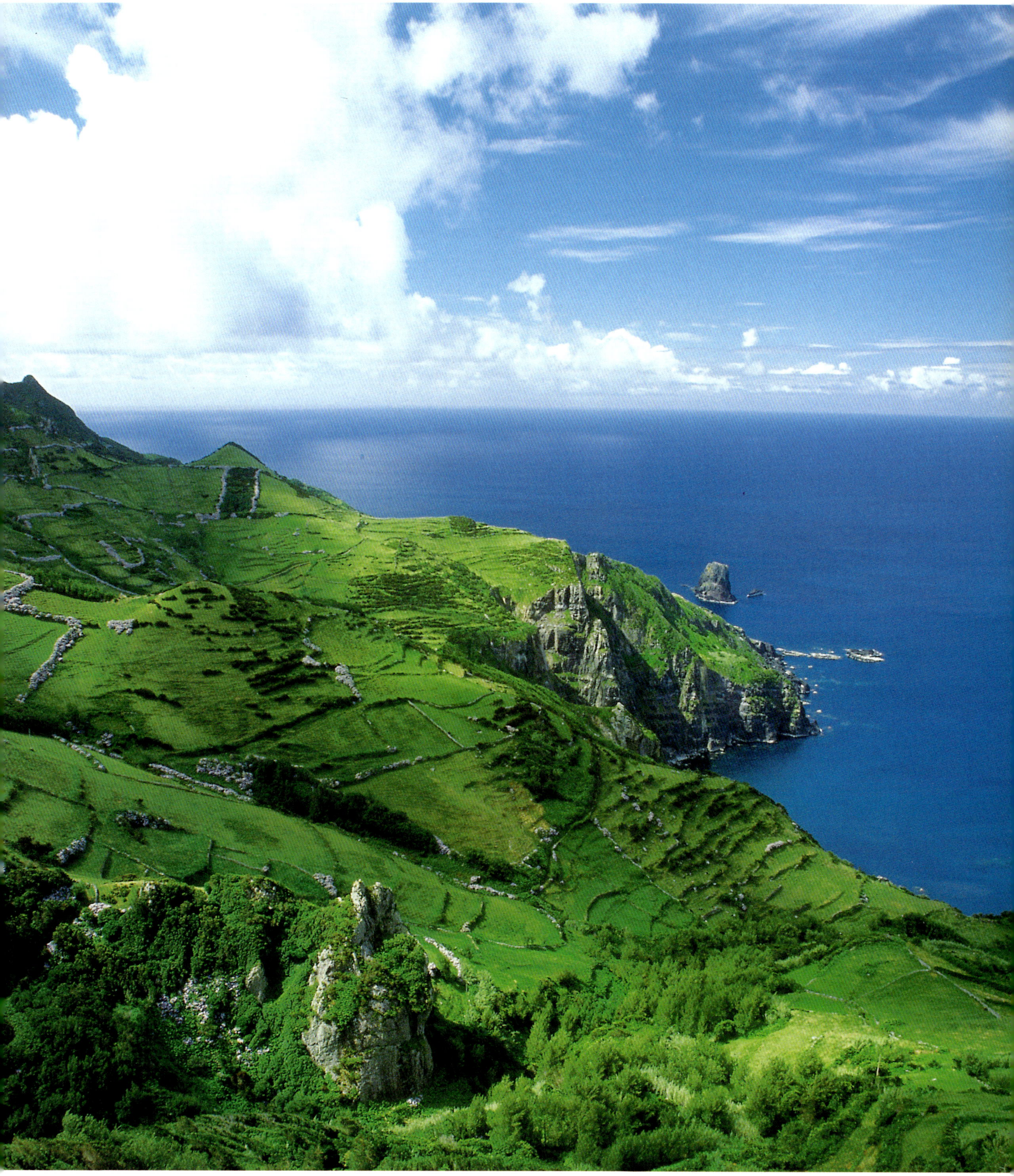

64 top At Câmara de Lobos, one of the towns on Madeira, they have for centuries fished black scabbard fish, one of the island's traditional dishes. The coastal scenery, gentle and bright, was immortalised in famous pictures painted by Winston Churchill, a frequent visitor to these parts.

64 bottom Funchal is the capital of Madeira; despite conserving major traces of its past, the town now has modern buildings and good tourist amenities.

65 top Much of the mountainous territory of Madeira has been turned into terraces, used to cultivate the grapes that produce the famous liqueur-like wine that bears the island's name. Madeira does not export wine alone: it is also famous for lace, basket-ware and tropical flowers and fruit.

65 bottom Around Pico Ruivo and Paul da Serra, the mountainous area inland of Madeira regains its original appearance; the first visitors were greeted by a thick forest and called the island Madeira, "wood" in Portuguese.

66-67 The coast of Porto Moniz, the second largest town on Madeira, is exposed to the winds and tides of the north, and is jagged and full of inlets. Nature seems to have delighted in creating striking views: mountains sheer above the sea and rivers of petrified lava, eroded by the sea to form the so-called "pools", natural basins that hold and heat the sea water.

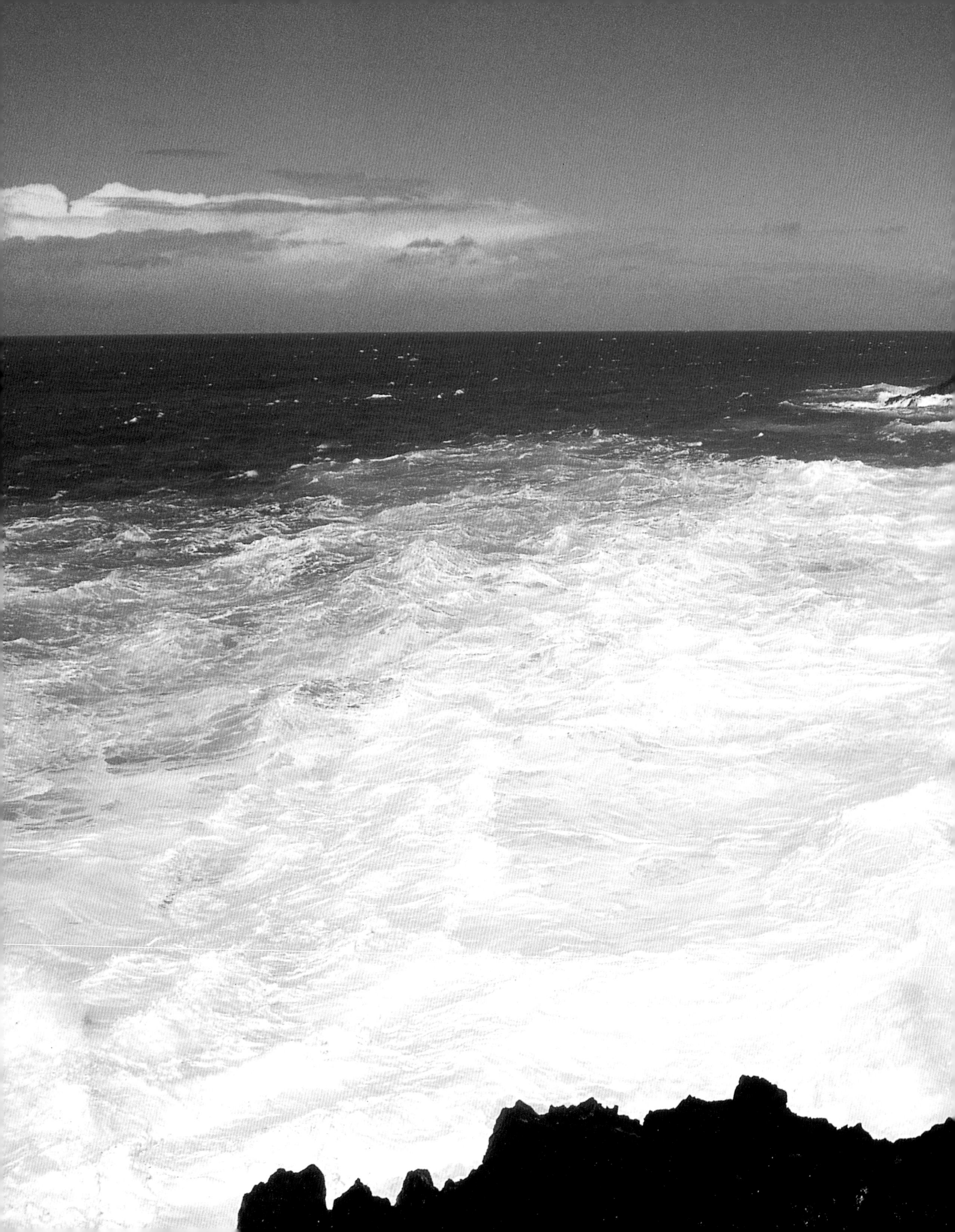

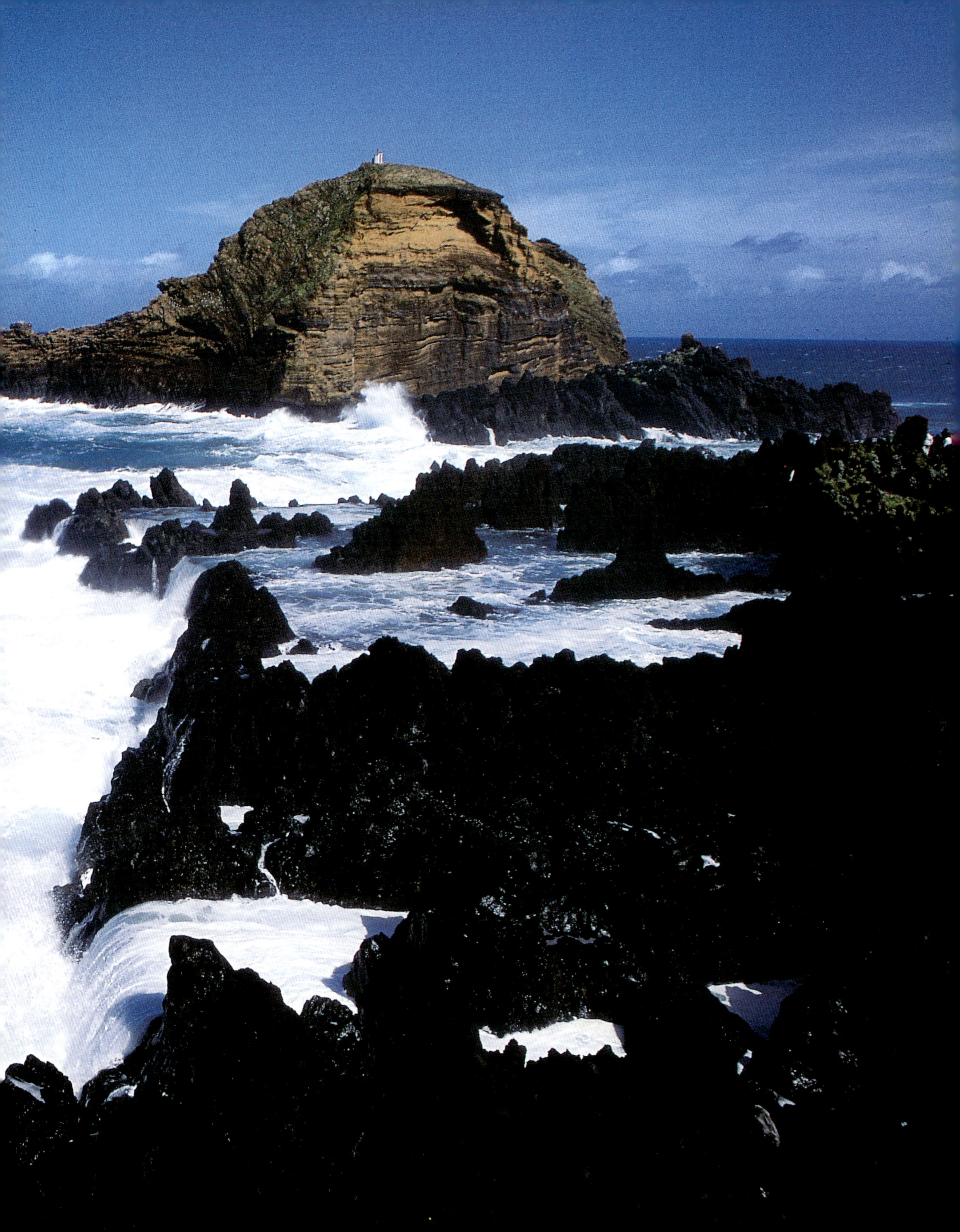

The atmosphere of the metropolises

68 top The castle of São Jorge commands views of the Baixa, or lower town, the district of Lisbon razed to the ground by an earthquake in 1755 and reconstructed in just under 30 years in the French style in vogue at the time. Wide thoroughfares, impressive palaces with characteristic amaranth-coloured roofs replaced what remained of the old Moorish district, that worst hit by the catastrophe.

68 bottom The Aqueduto das Aguas Livres crosses the entire Alcantara valley, on the edge of the Portuguese capital. It took more than three centuries to construct and definitively resolved Lisbon's recurrent problem: water shortage.

69 The monastery of Batalha combines the giddily spectacular Gothic with the sublime abundance of "chaotic" Manueline, a style custom-made for Portugal's golden era. The towers, spires and ogival vaults of the monastery symbolise earthly aspirations to rise to the heavenly, while shells, nets and hawsers recall the adventurous, oceanic dimensions of man's great exploits.

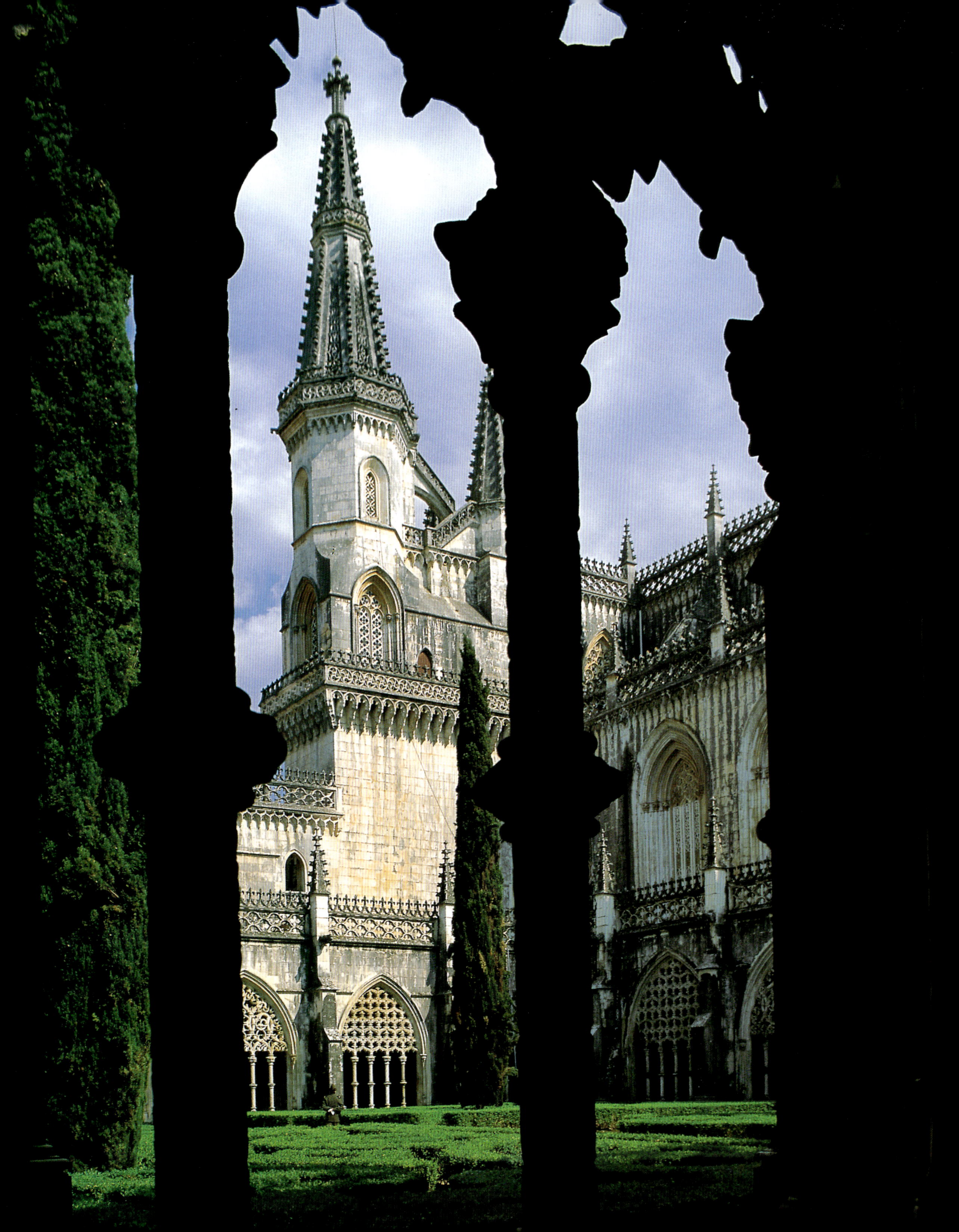

70

Lisbon, the nostalgic capital

70-71 There are many definitions of the Portuguese capital, and each is true: Lisbon is a city of a thousand faces, provincial and international, rich and poor. The signs of its grandeur are seen in the beauty of the Baixa (centre), in the friezes adorning the Arch of Triumph (top left), the military museum (top right) or the entrance to the railway station (bottom right), as too in the Padrão dos Descobrimentos (bottom left), the monument that more than any other celebrates the golden era and the country's desire to relaunch itself.

72-73 *Praça da Figueira, in Lisbon, is an example of the urbanistic concept dear to the Marques de Pombal, the man who started the recovery of the old centre after the earthquake: at the centre of the square, where the covered market used to stand, is the monument to João I, the king who won independence from Castile.*

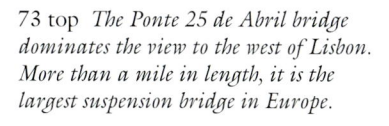

73 top *The Ponte 25 de Abril bridge dominates the view to the west of Lisbon. More than a mile in length, it is the largest suspension bridge in Europe.*

73 centre *Created in the first decades of this century, the Parque Eduardo VII owes its name to an act of courtesy towards the British king who visited Lisbon in 1903. It is the largest park in the city.*

73 bottom *Like Belém, Alfama too survived the earthquake and thus conserves many traits of the Arab district of the past. Inhabited since the Middle Ages by fishermen, craftsmen and small traders, it later became the district of sailors and prostitutes. Today it is the living model of the poorer part of Lisbon.*

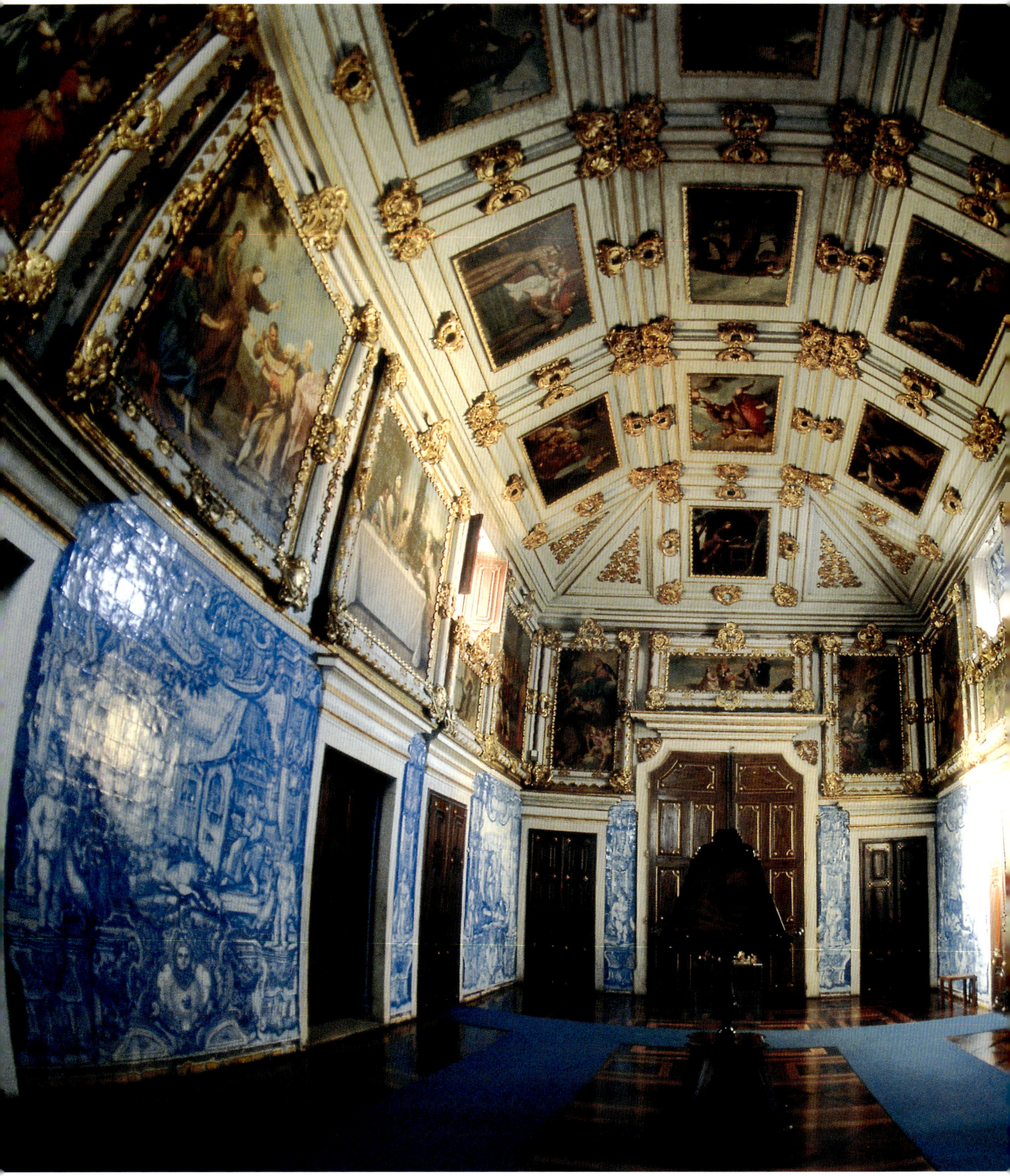

74-75 *The history of azulejos, decorative tiles that have over the years become the most original form of Portuguese art, is told in the Convento da Madre de Deus, since the 1800s the home of the Museu Nacional do Azulejo. The museum records the evolution of* azulejos, *from the early Arab pieces of the 16th century to the later Flemish-worked tiles. The art of the* azulejos *grew so rapidly that in the 17th century the fashion of* tapetes *(seen in blue in the photograph) emerged, with entire walls being tiled; the following century it became customary practice to clad every valuable surface (churches, fountains, stairs) with coloured tiles.*

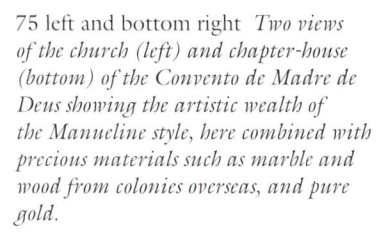

75 left and bottom right *Two views of the church (left) and chapter-house (bottom) of the Convento de Madre de Deus showing the artistic wealth of the Manueline style, here combined with precious materials such as marble and wood from colonies overseas, and pure gold.*

75 top right *Built in the late 14th century, the Igreja do Carmo is the monument to the disaster that changed the history of Portugal, the earthquake. It collapsed on All Saints Day in 1755 and was intentionally not rebuilt as a tribute to the horror of that tragic day. It houses the Museu Arqueologico and, during good weather, open air concerts.*

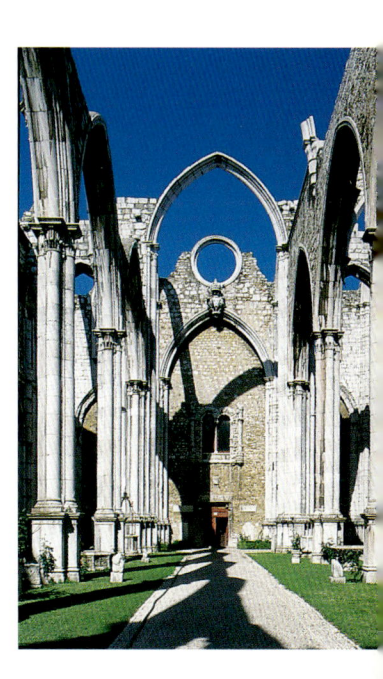

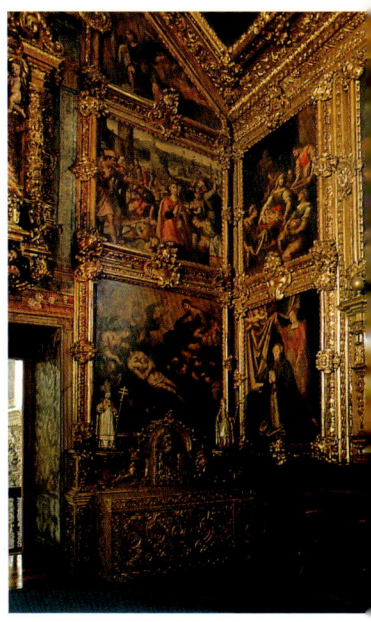

76 top The Palácio Nacional de Ajuda was to replace the royal castle destroyed by the earthquake of 1755 but construction problems delayed its completion by more than a century: the finished monumental complex is smaller than originally intended and the façade has the clearly Neo-classical appearance typical of Romanticism.

76 centre Along with the Teatro Nacional Dona Maria II, the Teatro São Carlos is where the opera and ballet lovers of the Portuguese capital meet; spectacular, majestic and blessed with uncommon acoustic qualities, this theatre offers the best of the European programme to Portuguese enthusiasts. The theatre, opera and, more generally, artistic seasons are busy and much appreciated in a city with illustrious traditions that sees the promotion of culture as a policy for advancement.

76 bottom Opened in 1962 in the Palácio Pimenta, the Museu da Cidade provides visitors with a historical perspective of the history of Lisbon. Of particular interest is the room dedicated to the earthquake, containing a model of the city as it was before that fateful day in 1755.

76-77 *The interior of the elegant and opulent Palácio Nacional de Ajuda shows the signs of the royal family's passage. The building was however inhabited by the monarchs for just 50 years, between 1861 and 1910; after that date the apartments were opened to the public, turned into auditoriums or used for cultural exhibitions. As well as precious furnishings and tapestries it contains 20 marble statues made in the 19th century by sculptors of the Mafra school.*

78 top Among the countless museums of Lisbon, the Museu Nacional dos Coches (museum of coaches) always arouses much curiosity. Created at the wishes of the Portuguese royal family in the early 1900s, the museum offers the most spectacular collection of ancient coaches and vintage cars in Europe.

78 centre Housed in a west wing of the Mosteiro dos Jerónimos, the Museu da Marinha was founded in 1863; the major attractions include numerous models of fishing and warships, original nautical charts and the Santa Clara seaplane, the first plane to fly across the Atlantic, between Lisbon and Rio de Janeiro. Impressive statues are dedicated to the leading figures in Portuguese maritime history: the most important of course is the "father" of the colonial adventure, Henry the Navigator (at the centre of the picture) who founded the school of navigation at Sagres.

78 bottom As well as a rich collection of azulejos and panels portraying some of the major battles in Portuguese history, the Museu Militar – seen here is a room of clearly pompous Baroque inspiration – possesses a rich collection of Portuguese, French, English, Spanish, Dutch and Arab fire-arms.

79 The Museu da Marinha exhibits numerous works dedicated to the kings and navigators that made the history of Portugal. The pictures show two noblemen who governed the overseas provinces: João de Castro (left) and Francisco de Almedia (right), governor of India in the early 1500s.

G.ᴿ DO: IOÃO DE CASTRO SOS EDE O AO G.ʳ MARTIÃO DESBARATOV
E DIO TODO O PODER DE CÃ BAIA PRESẼTOV BATALHA
A ELREI DE BAROCHE E DESTROIO TODAS VA COSTA
EA DE ADIL XA. DESBAR ATOV SEVS CAPITAĨS E SAL
SETE. Ẽ TROV TREHŨ FÃ DO Ẽ GOA.

V EO DO ROA NO DE 4 S. GOVERNO V 2. ANOS E 8.
MESES FA LECEO Ẽ GOA C O M MAIS 1 ANOS
CÕ TITVLO DE VISO REI

GVOVERNA DOR DA ÍM
DIA. D. FRAN CISCO E ALMEIDA
ANO 1505

O VICE REI D. FRAN CISCO DE AL
MEIDA, O PRIMEI RO QUE PASSOU A EST
ESTADO COM O DITO TÍTU LO DEPOIS D
DESCOBRIMENTO DA INDIA, C HEGOU A ELL
NO ANNO DE 1505, E GOVER NOU ATE 18 D
NOVE MBRO DE 1509

80 top Details of the cloister of the Mosteiro dos Jerónimos reveal distinctive Manueline traits: complex ornamentation of pillars and vaults, bas-reliefs covering the columns, an evident mixture of styles, the double two-light arches with typically oriental decorations.

80 bottom The Mosteiro dos Jerónimos is probably the most famous monument in Lisbon: having survived the 18th-century earthquake, it shows to the full the style that marked Portugal's golden era, that of King Manuel I. The church of Santa Maria, in the centre of the monastery, is a resumé of this art and, in a broad sense, of Portuguese history too. It is a blend of the most diverse forms and with varied contributions, a tribute to the cosmopolitanism of the Manueline empire. Symbols of seafaring exploits are mixed with the customary signs of Catholic devotion, Arab decorations (clearly visible in this picture of the vault) mix with the typically western.

81 top With his naval adventures, Vasco da Gama, the great navigator and symbol of the golden era, earned himself eternal rest within the walls of the Mosteiro dos Jerónimos; his tomb is visited by thousands of people every year.

81 bottom This picture taken from the River Tagus shows a fascinating view of the Praça do Imperio gardens, with the Fonte Luminosa and the splendid Mosteiro dos Jerónimos, perhaps the most beautiful monument in Lisbon.

80-81 The magnificent Mosteiro dos Jerónimos was made in pure Manueline style. Originally, the huge monastery of the Hieronymites stood on the banks of the Tagus; the works to construct the dock moved away the course of the river and led to the birth of the Praça do Imperio and the Avenida da India.

Queluz, the Portuguese Versailles

82 *The small village of Queluz (literally "what light!"), on the outskirts of Lisbon, boasts the summer residence of the royal Braganza family. Considered the "Portuguese Versailles", the Palácio Nacional de Queluz dates from the end of the 18th century and is now a splendid example of Rococo, albeit mixed in some parts with Neo-classical elements. The project was completed by two great 18th-century architects: Mateus Vicente de Oliveira and Jean-Baptiste Robillon.*

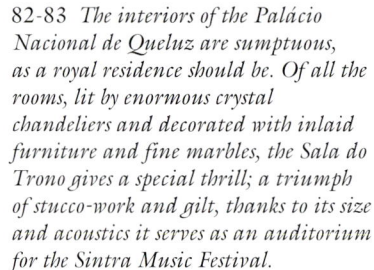

82-83 *The interiors of the Palácio Nacional de Queluz are sumptuous, as a royal residence should be. Of all the rooms, lit by enormous crystal chandeliers and decorated with inlaid furniture and fine marbles, the Sala do Trono gives a special thrill; a triumph of stucco-work and gilt, thanks to its size and acoustics it serves as an auditorium for the Sintra Music Festival.*

83

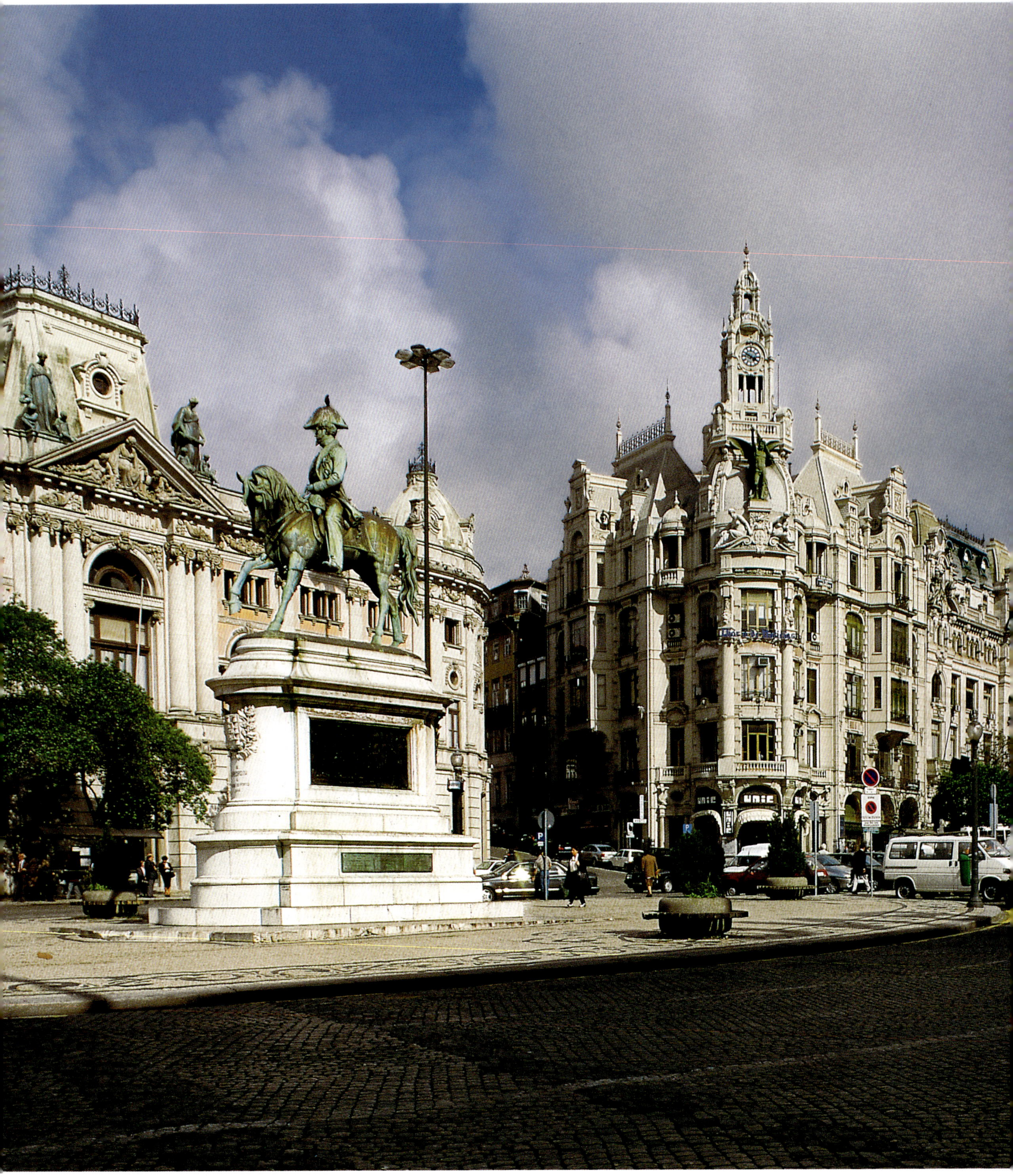

Oporto - labour is the creed

84-85 Praça da Libertade is the heart of Oporto, the capital of the north. An industrious and thriving city, its present well-being comes from the service sector and, at least in part, from sea trade. Elegant in the centre, chaotic on the outskirts, the city conserves the layout of a coastal city, descending from the vineyards of Gondomar towards the port of Leixões.

85 top The modern and well-equipped port of Leixões is Oporto's window on the world. The city is the second largest in Portugal (more than 350,000 inhabitants) and has maintained its traditional "privileged" trading relations with Latin America, England and France.

85 centre The Ribeira is the oldest district in Oporto, the only true urban legacy of the old port-city. The streets are narrow and filled with small shops, the houses higher and deeper than they are wide, with a minimal façade; here live the lower classes, just a stone's throw from the symbol of the city's wealth, the Stock Exchange.

85 bottom The famous barcos rebelos are still a common sight along the docks and under the Dom Luis iron bridge. These are traditional vessels used for centuries, until recent decades, to transport casks of wine on the Rio Douro, from the quintas where it is produced and aged to the wharves of Oporto where it is loaded on merchant ships that set sail for all parts of the world.

85

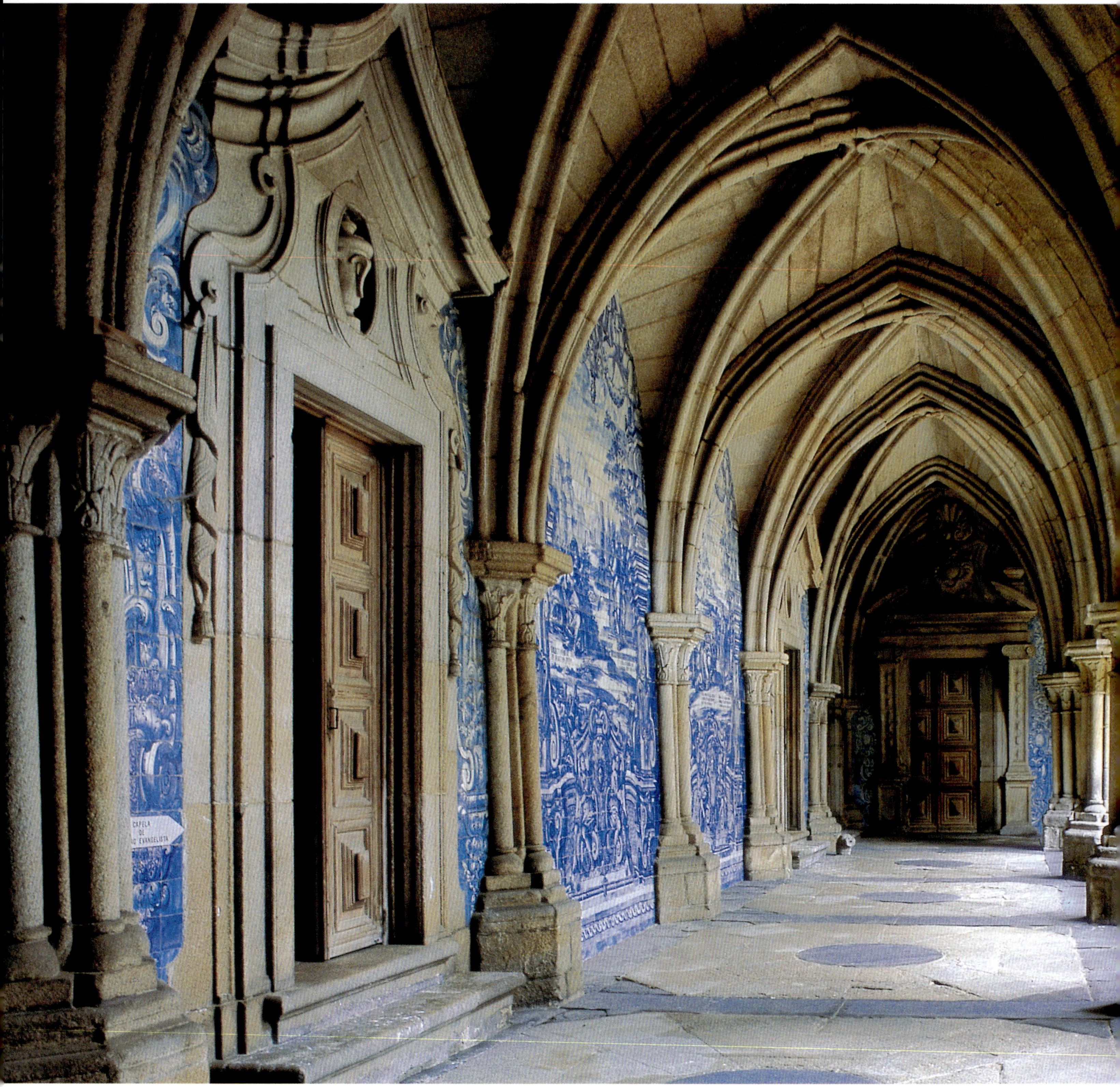
CAPELA
DE
EVANGELISTA

86-87 The cathedral of Oporto (the Sé), built in the 12th century in Romanesque style, has been repeatedly tampered with but conserves the stern appearance of religious buildings constructed in that period, more fortresses than churches. Along the walls of the cloister (in the picture) are 18th-century tapetes *depicting the "Song of Songs" and the "Metamorphoses".*

87 top The hall of the railway station of São Bento in Oporto was embellished in 1916 with numerous azulejos *portraying scenes of everyday Portuguese life in past centuries.*

87 bottom This view of the Sé of Oporto highlights the type and number of decorative additions made over the centuries in the most diverse styles to the original Romanesque style of the church. Numerous parts of the cathedral were built when Manueline style was at its peak, as is shown by this column in the square in front of the basilica.

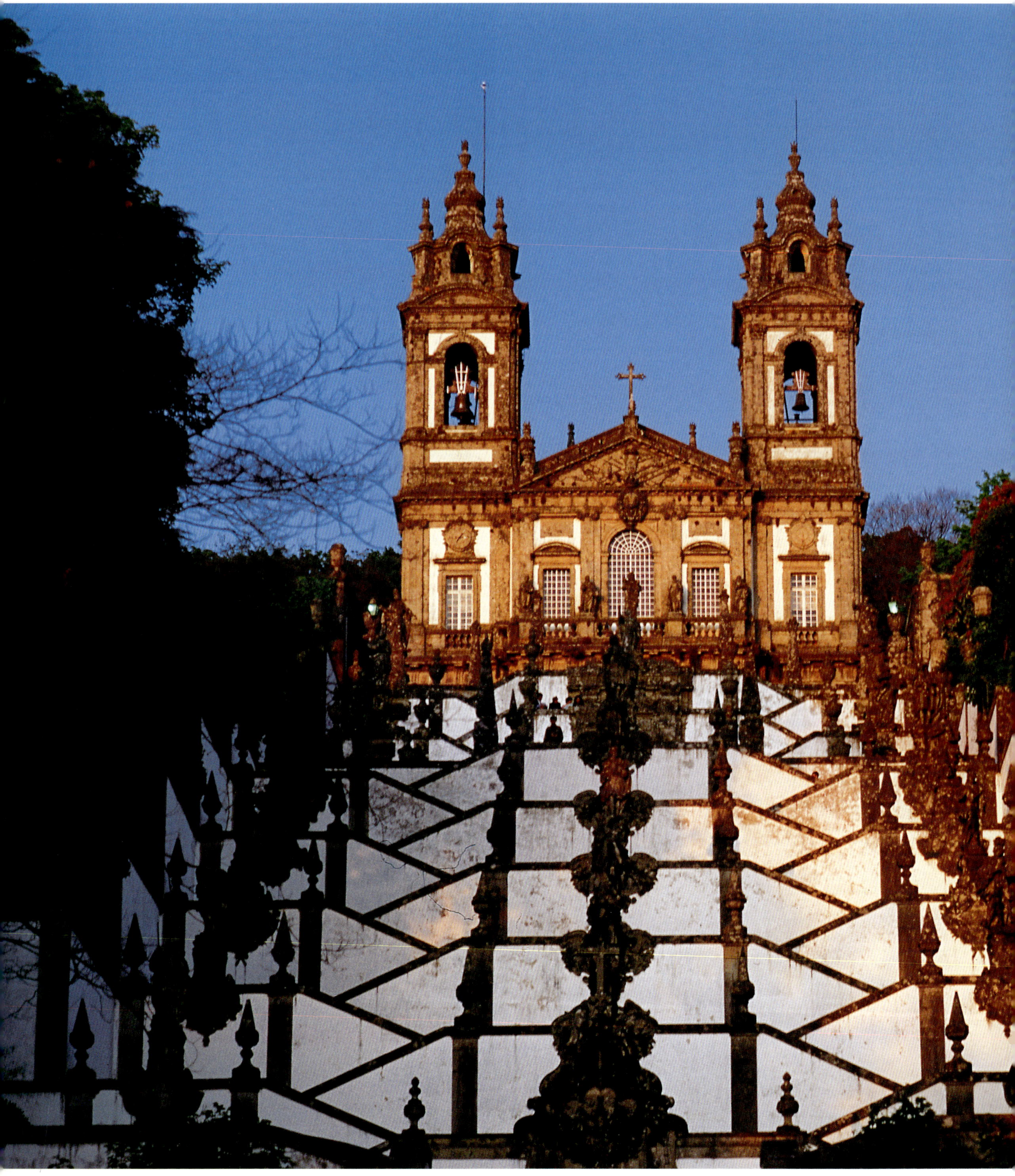

Braga, the town of prayer

88-89 An unusual double flight of Baroque steps ascends the hill dominated by the sanctuary of Bom Jesus do Monte, situated at the centre of a splendid park much-loved by the people of Braga.

89 top Braga is a dynamic and modern city that has not forgotten its past. Full churches and sanctuaries are indication of the "religious" inclinations of this town set in the heart of the Minho; the elegant, newly-restored buildings and well-tended Baroque gardens show instead that the money of the economic boom of recent years has been well spent.

89 centre Praça da República is the urban and social heart of Braga where the city movida animates the porticoes and paved square. This is a relatively recent phenomenon, since at the beginning of this century the famous Spanish writer Miguel de Unamuno, when a guest here, complained that the streets of the pious Braga were deserted from dusk to dawn.

89 bottom Perhaps for its strategic position (the five most important roads in Portugal passed through Bragara Augusta, as it was called), perhaps because it had an archbishopric as early as the 12th century, Braga became a sort of Portuguese Rome and the powerful local clergy has left a splendid artistic heritage, from numerous monasteries to an interminable string of churches and chapels.

Sintra, a pearl set in the woods

90 top left Sintra boasts the most unusual castle in the land, the Palácio da Pena: a singular ensemble of domes, drawbridges, minarets and towers in various mixed styles – along the lines of the Bavarian castles – set atop the highest mountain in the area.

90 centre left A few miles from the Palácio Nacional da Pena stands the Quinta de Monserrate, a 19th-century villa, in Moorish style, set in English gardens filled with subtropical plants and tree-ferns.

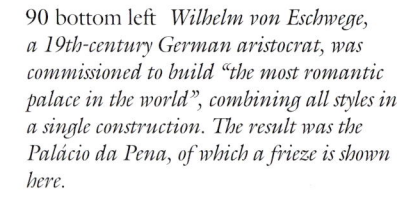

90 bottom left Wilhelm von Eschwege, a 19th-century German aristocrat, was commissioned to build "the most romantic palace in the world", combining all styles in a single construction. The result was the Palácio da Pena, of which a frieze is shown here.

90 right The architect who designed the Palácio Nacional da Pena used decorative elements peculiar to Lisbon: the picture shows the diamond-pointed rustication originally used for the Casa dos Bicos, applied here to the wall of one of the entrance portals.

90-91 The Palácio Nacional da Pena, set in a fairy-tale park on the Serra da Sintra, was for many years the summer residence of the royal family: only the flight of the Braganza family brought the monarchical history of Portugal and the castle to a close.

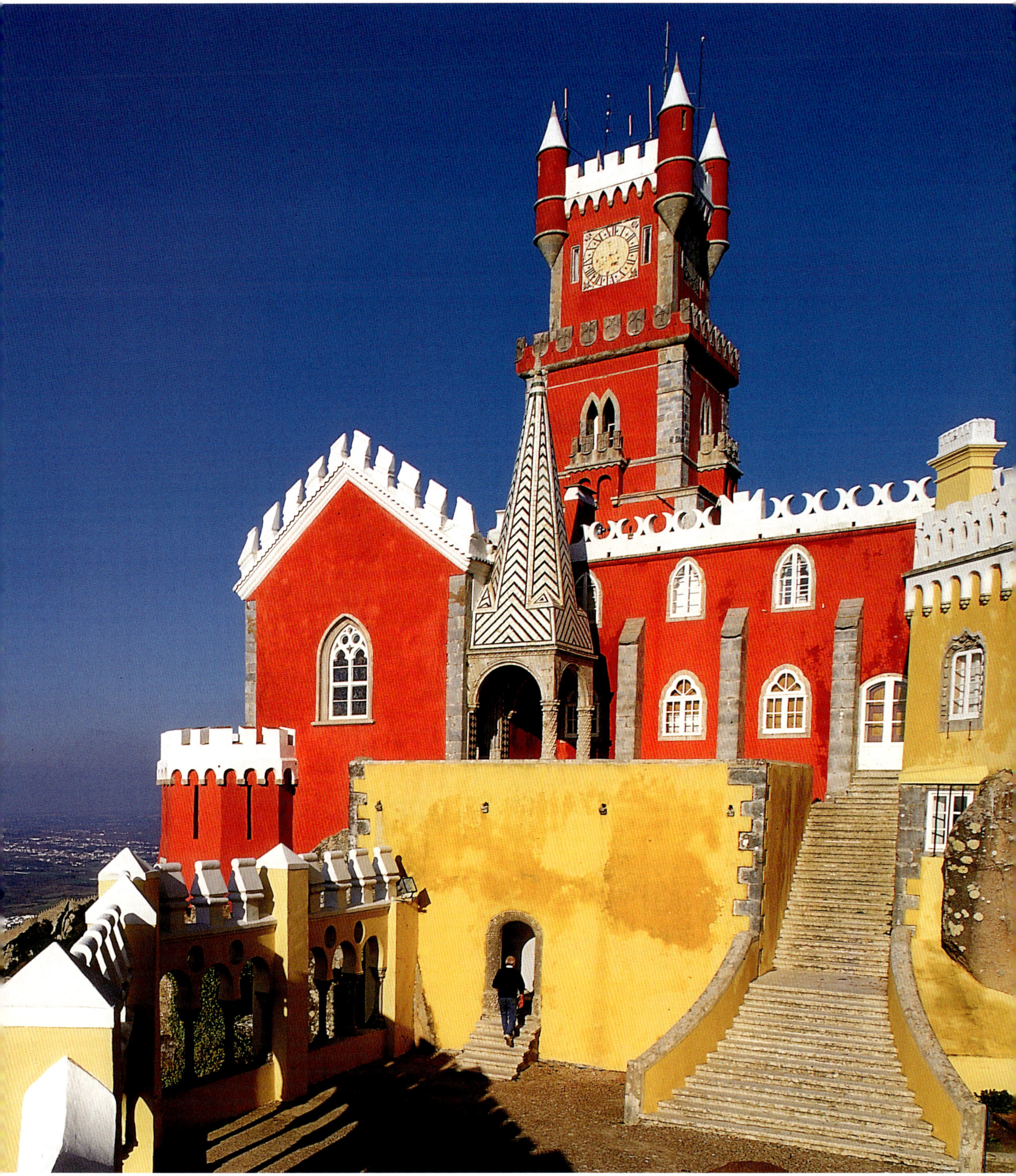

92 top Nearly 1,640 feet high, looming above Sintra, the Castelo dos Mouros was built between the 8th and 9th centuries. Of the original construction only the battlements and towers have survived.

92 bottom A visit to the Palácio Nacional reveals several pleasant surprises. The furnishings, the wooden, marble or azulejos panelling (present in nearly all the rooms), the precious floors and the very history intrinsic to its every part blend to create an extraordinary atmosphere.

93 top The Palácio Nacional (known as Paço Real to avoid confusion with the Palácio Nacional da Pena) dominates the skyline of Sintra, a splendid town immersed in the fascinating, wooded Serra of the same name. The main body of the building was erected in the 15th century and the two huge, conical chimneys that used to be part of the royal kitchen, added in the 17th century, are seen from afar.

93 bottom The Sala dos Brasoes (i.e. blazons, also known as the stag room) is one of the most impressive rooms in the Palácio Nacional of Sintra. The ceiling is an octagonal wooden dome, painted in the early 1500s; prancing stags support the coats of arms of the noble Portuguese families. At the centre of the dome is the blazon of Manuel I. The walls of the room are lined with azulejos *depicting hunting scenes.*

Inland Treasures

94 top right *Like many of the constructions of the period (twelfth century), the Sé Velha, the old cathedral of Coimbra, resembles a fortress more than a church. Only the Porta Especiosa and the belfry adorned with Renaissance motifs differ from the somber style of the rest of the building.*

94 top left *Declared a national monument, Obidos is one of the pearls of the Costa da Prata. Entirely fortified, it is also delicately beautiful in parts.*

94 bottom left *The fortifications (the picture shows the castle built in 1171 by the Templars at Amoural, at the confluence of the Tagus and the Rio Zêzere) erected over the centuries all over Portugal bear witness to a troubled history plagued by war. After the fall of the Roman empire, the country was first invaded by the Visigoths and then the Moors. The oldest Portuguese castles, built at strategic points in the mountainous regions and the Asturias, date from that time and from the centuries of the reconquest. The Castilian-style constructions date from the late-Middle Ages, when at the cost of long and ferocious wars, the Portuguese won independence from Spain.*

95 *Tomar, built in the Nabao Valley, in the heart of Estremadura, is the city of the Templars. The whole town is dominated by the great convent-castle of the Knights Templar, surrounded by a forest of pine trees and the home of two orders (Templars and Order of Christ).*

96-97 *The famous Wine Route, the memorable road along the Rio Douro has one obligatory stop: the Solar de Mateus. A baroque mansion built in the eighteenth century at Vila Real by the counts of Mateus, the solar is the emblem of a wine empire famous throughout the world. The wine made with the grapes of this region is called Mateus and carries the distinctive façade of the owner's villa on the label.*

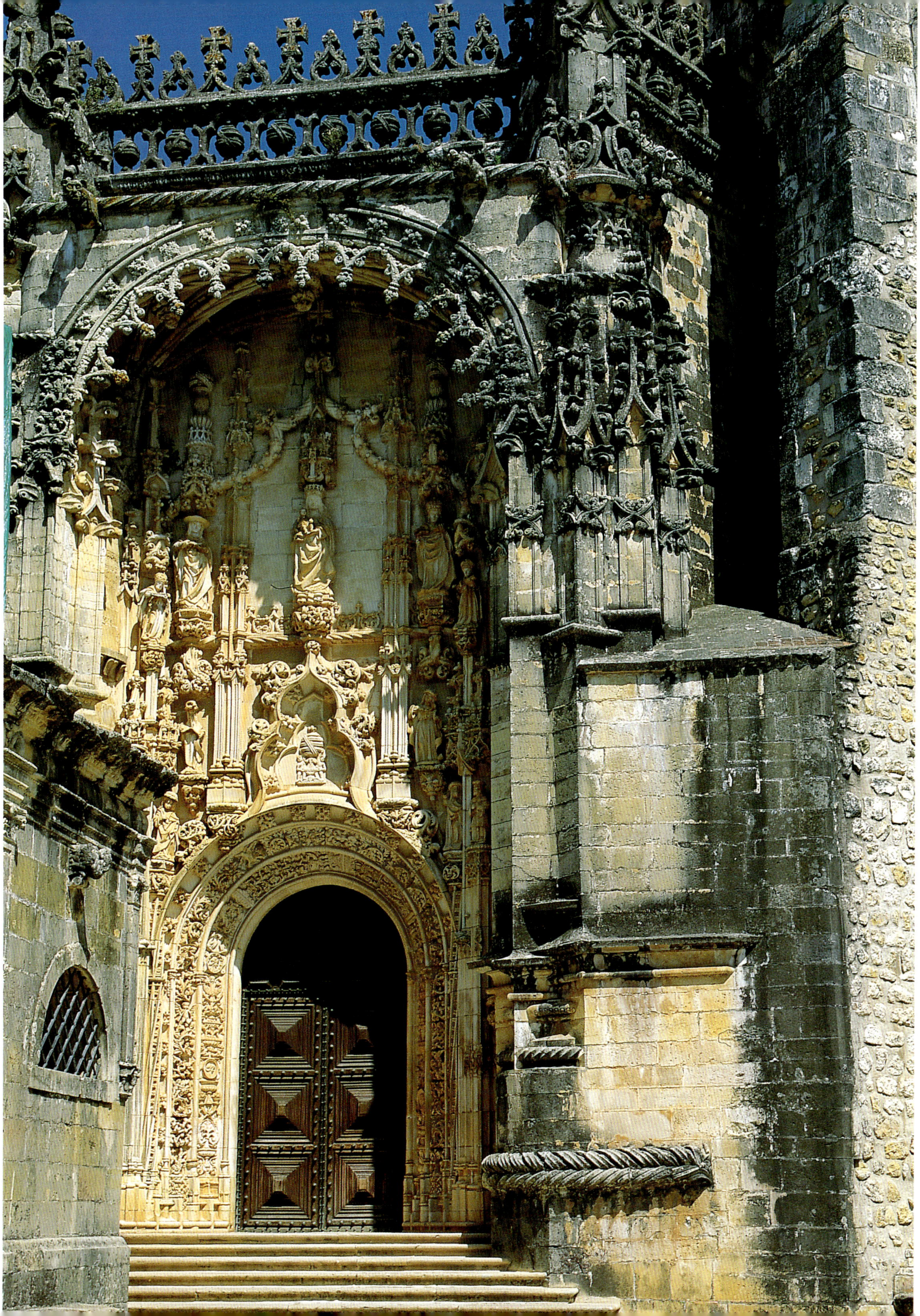

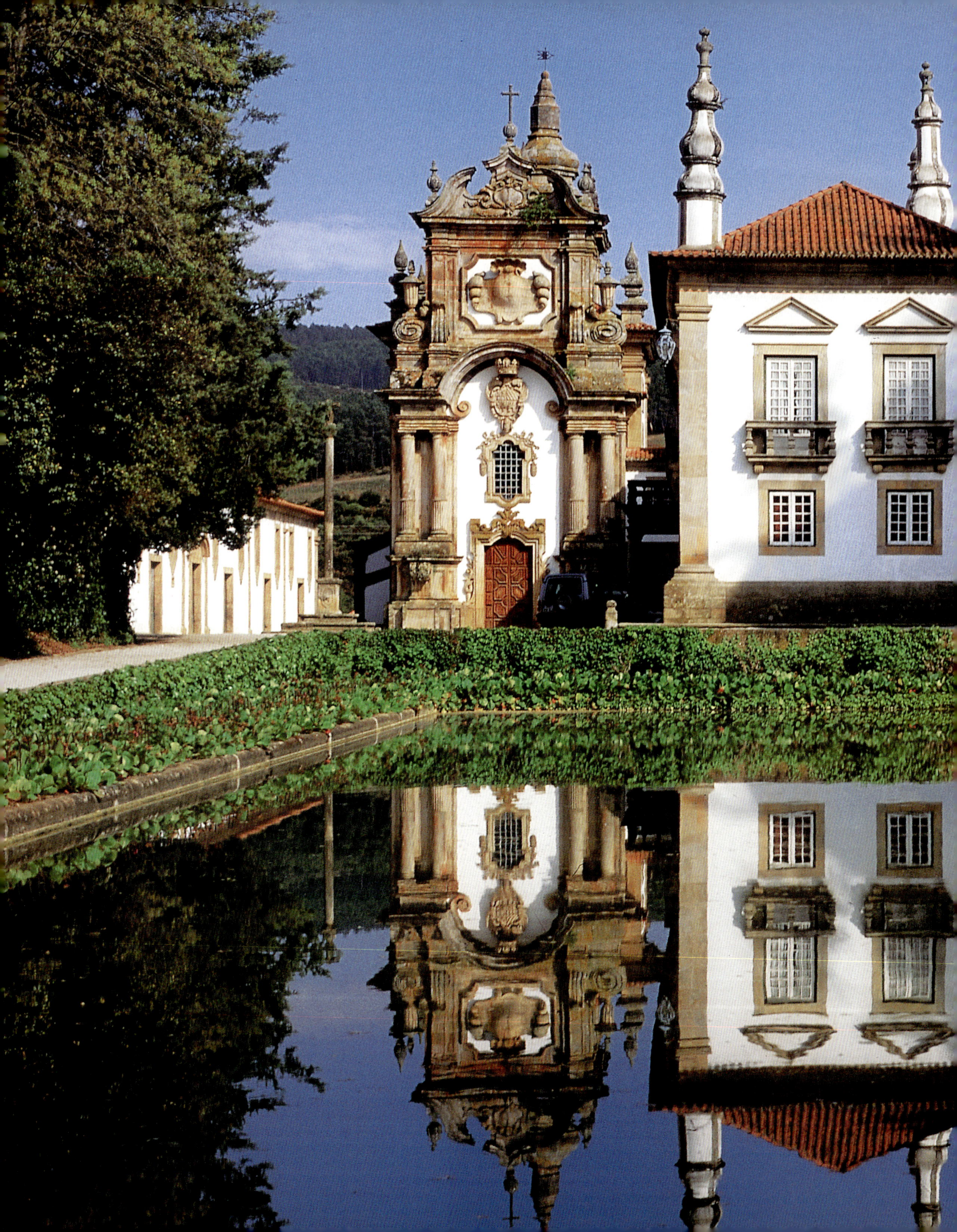

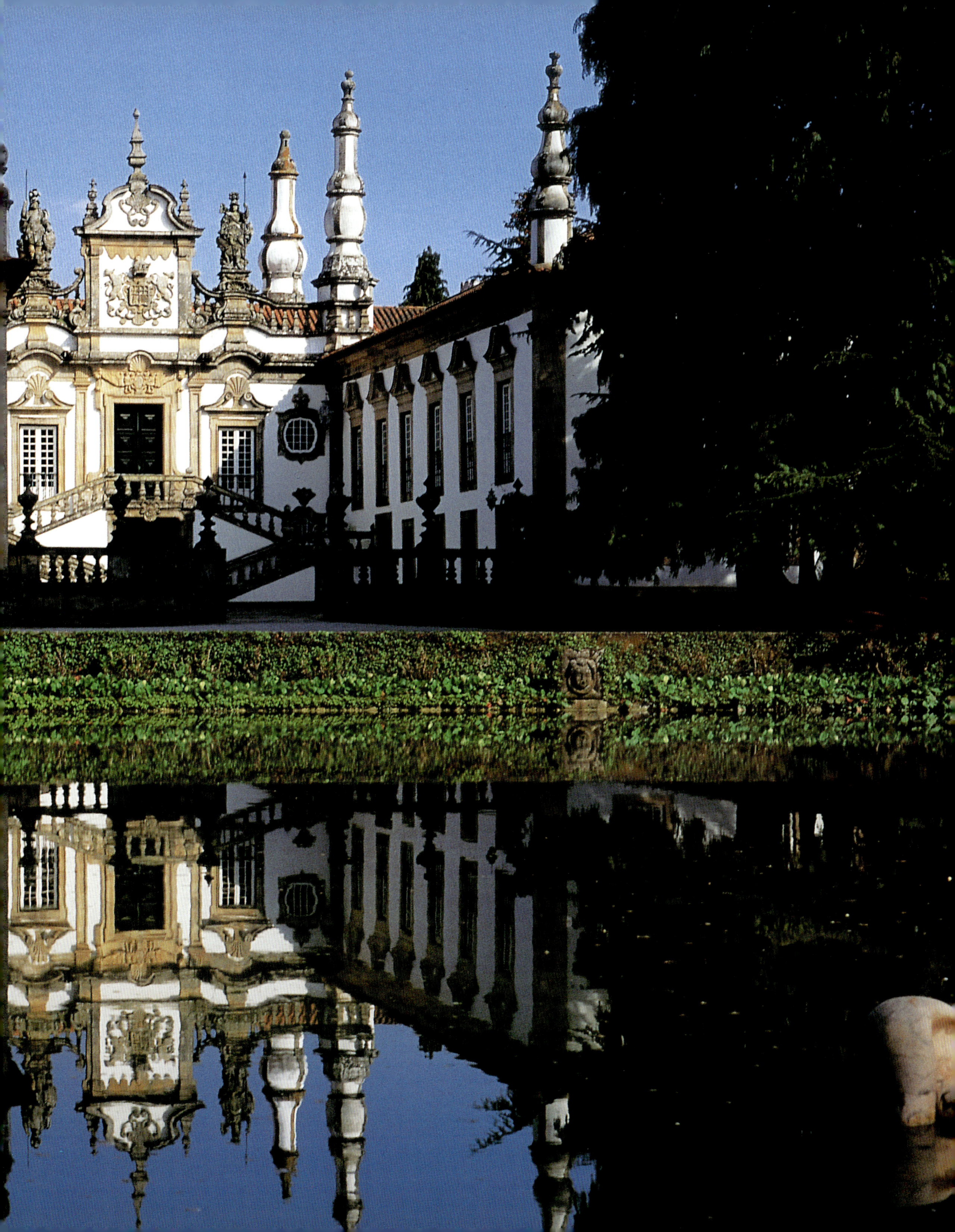

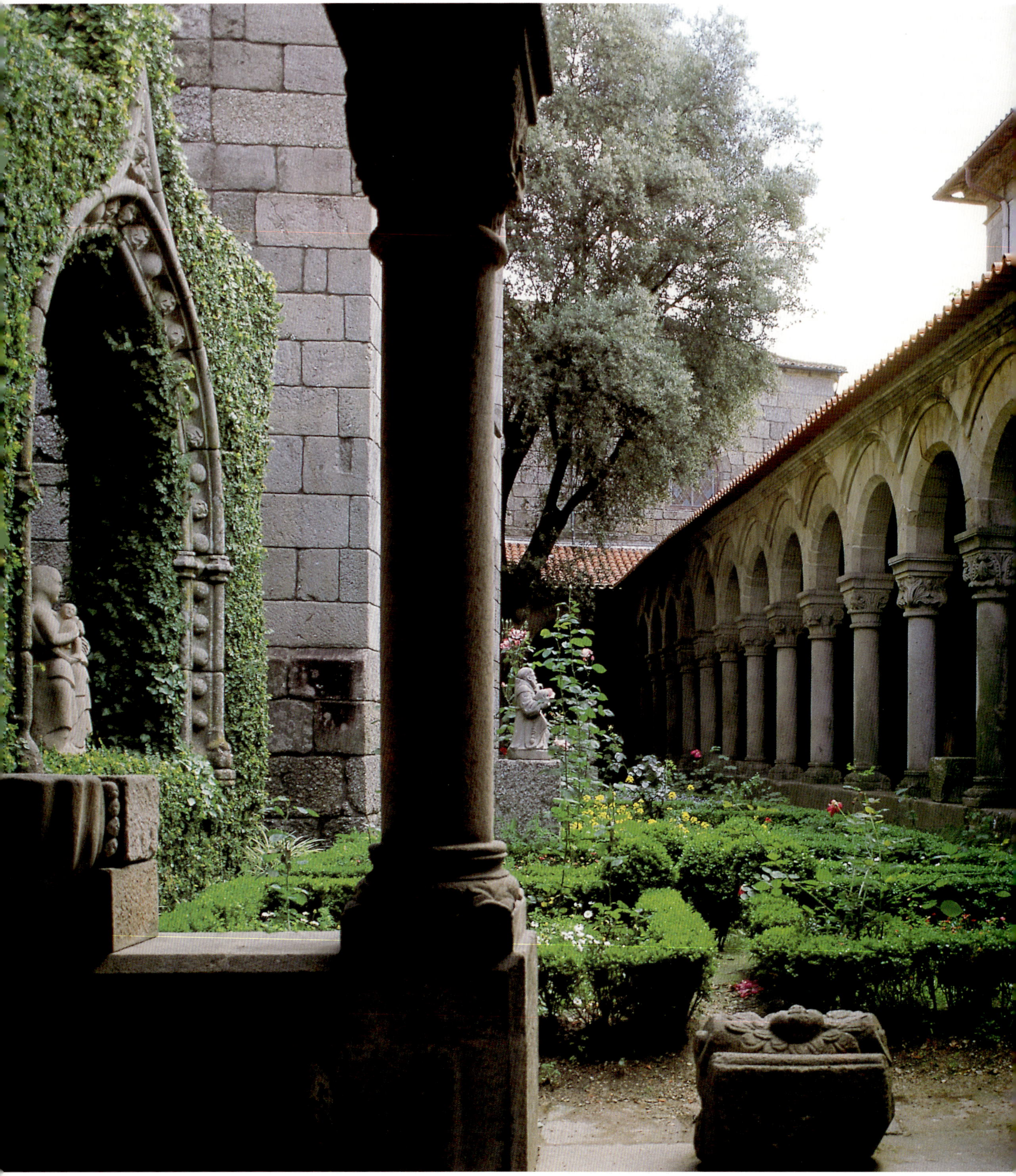

Guimarães, the cradle of the Braganza family

98-99 *The cloister of the Museu Alberto Sampaio in Guimarães consists of a beautiful loggia and a secluded courtyard with French garden flaunting the characteristic Manueline ornamental motifs. The museum is one of the most important in Portugal and houses the treasure of the Dukes of Braganza – precious silver objects and a portable altar decorated in bas-relief.*

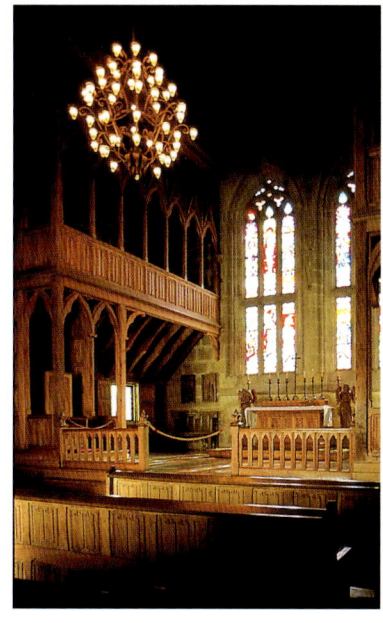

99 left *The chapel of the Palace of the Dukes of Braganza is a fine example of Gothic with just a few Manueline additions. The picture also shows the high pointed stained glass windows that illuminate the two wooden women's galleries.*

99 right *The Palace of the Dukes of Braganza (top, with its characteristic chimneys) and the castle (bottom, seen here are the towers, walls and entrance) share a sombre and essential style and are the two most impressive buildings of Guimarães, the home of the Braganza family.*

"Buen retiro" of the Mascarenhas

100 top Situated on the edge of the Parque Florestal de Monsanto, on the outskirts of Lisbon, the Palácio dos Marques de Fronteira was built for Dom João Mascarenhas in Italian Renaissance style. Members of the noble family still live here and stroll through extensive and splendid gardens. Some of the rooms in the palace and the gardens, famous for the decorative plant sculptures, splendid azulejos and the numerous Neo-classical works, have for some years been open to visitors accompanied by a guide.

100 bottom The Palácio dos Marques de Fronteira is renowned more for its beautiful gardens than for the design of the building; the garden of Venus and the Italian garden, designed in the 17th century, are particularly attractive. A visit to the park is like taking a stroll through an open-air museum: paths, grottoes and terraces are lined with azulejos *painted by the masters of the Seicento and small niches house busts of sovereigns and reproductions of classical statues.*

101 The treasure of the gardens of Palácio dos Marques de Fronteira is the Kings' Gallery, a row of knights all portrayed on blue and white tapetes *of* azulejos. *Two staircases rise around the Moorish-style pool allowing the masterpiece to be admired from several angles. The majolicas that adorn the gardens, especially those in the Kings' Gallery, are considered the highest expression of this art: the refined motifs were painted in two colours for the first time on glazed tiles.*

Batalha, stone tracery

102 *Along with the Mosteiro dos Jerónimos of Lisbon, the monastery of Santa Maria da Vitoria in Batalha, is unanimously considered a masterpiece of Manueline art. Built at the end of the 14th century in Gothic style – of which clear traces remain in the façade (top right) and in the ogival arches of the interior (left) – mixed with Renaissance elements, it was completed after two centuries in keeping with the style in vogue at the time, i.e. to the highest Manueline standards. The mixture of styles has produced effects of remarkable beauty, as in the case of the Capela do Fundador (bottom right) with its pointed Gothic arches closed by a splendid star vault of Manueline inspiration.*

103 *The Claustro Real is the heart of the monastery of Santa Maria da Vitoria. Designed, as is the building's main body, in Gothic style, it was tampered with during the golden era; to instil in those observing it the sense of Portugal's new colonial wealth, the ogival windows were given stone gratings, defined by some as "embroidered stone".*

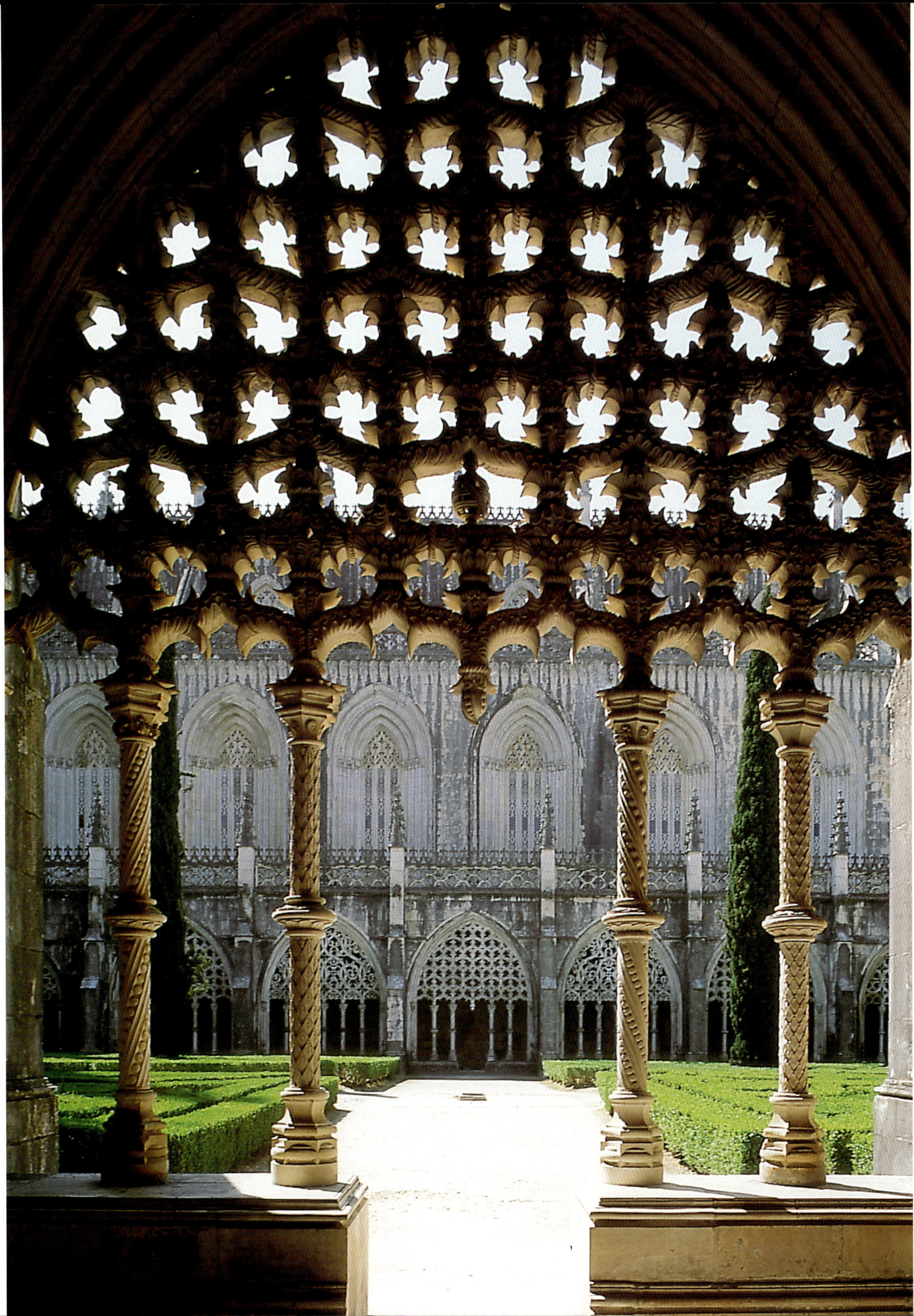

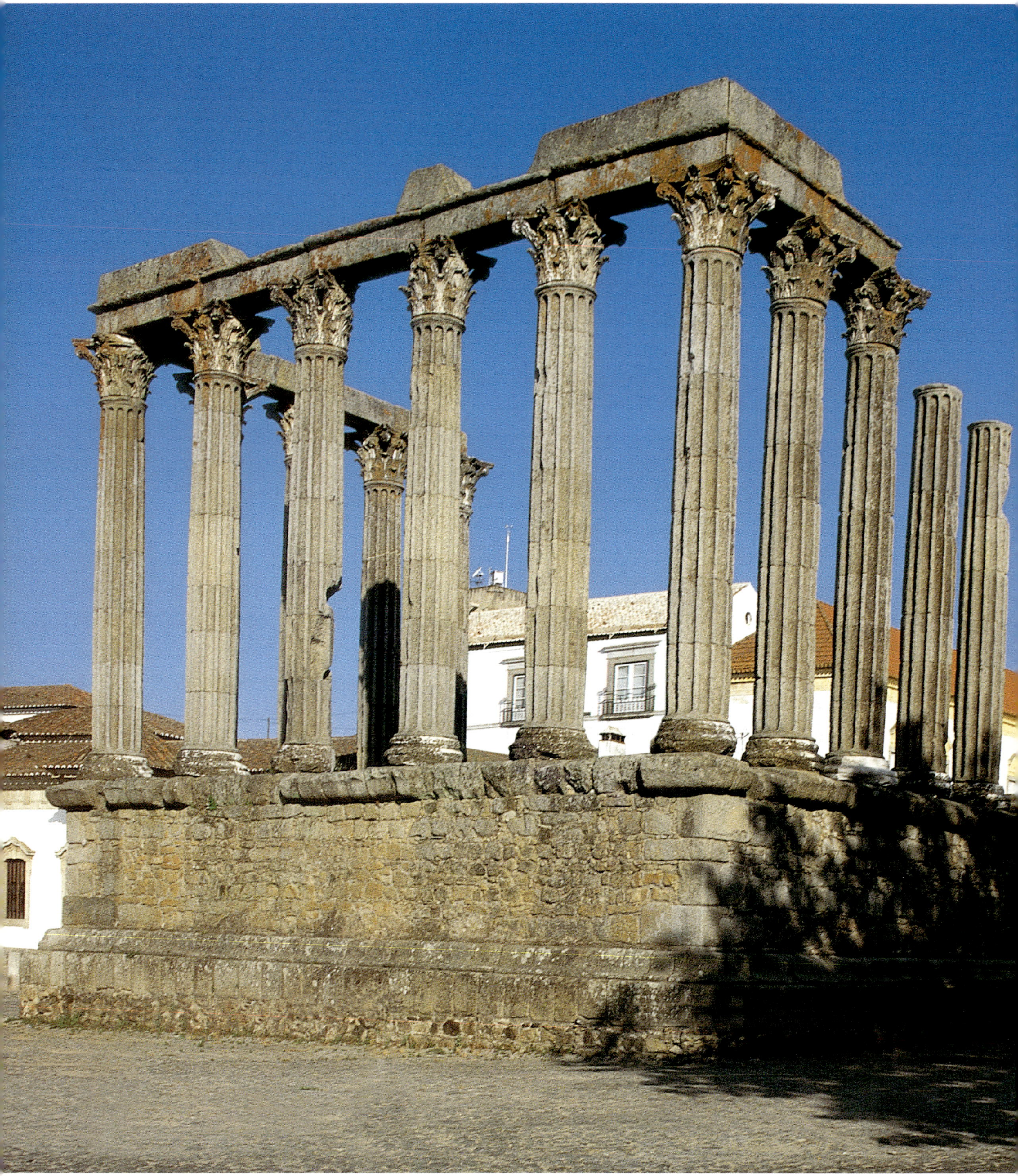

Following Caesar

*104-105 and 105 right Valuable evidence of the passage of the Romans has been found in archaeological sites on the planicies (plains), the region between the River Tagus and the Spanish border. Nearly all the traces of the Roman era were found after the 1755 earthquake, so violent that it literally lifted the lid off the places now excavated.
The Roman temple of Evora, a town on the planicies particularly prosperous in imperial times, is one of the most famous and interesting monuments to have survived the passing centuries and repeated interventions from the Middle Ages on. A Corinthian-style peripteral temple, dedicated to Diana or more probably the worship of the emperor, this is one of the best preserved of the peninsula; built in the town acropolis in the 2nd century BC, it was turned into a fortress in Mediaeval times and then restored to much of its former splendour in the late 19th century.*

105 left In 137 BC Lisbon and the rest of Portugal at last became part of the expanding Roman empire. After overcoming the local Iberian and Celtic peoples as well as, above all, as the Carthaginians, the Roman legions advanced from north to south, leaving traces of their passage everywhere: both outside the settlements, as shown by finds made all over the planicies (plains), and in the towns, which progressively incorporated the imperial remains. Excellent examples of this are two monuments in Evora: the Roman or Dona Isabel Gate (top), partially modified in subsequent eras, and the Rectangular Tower (bottom) a Mediaeval construction on a Roman base.

A thousand faces, a hundred races, one soul

106 top and 107 When the students of the famous university of Coimbra celebrate the end of the school year in May, they hold the Queima da Fitas, during which fresh graduates burn the symbols of the faculty after a lively procession. Then they party all night until dawn to the sound of fado.

106 bottom In Portugal, culture is not confined to museums or school. The Portuguese take pride in their being and appreciate all art forms that bring out their "essence". In Lisbon this diverges slightly with the capital's legitimate aspirations to be a European metropolis in the cultural sense. The result is a varied and lively cultural framework with exhibitions, theatre and opera seasons plus ballet or folk dancing every month of the year.

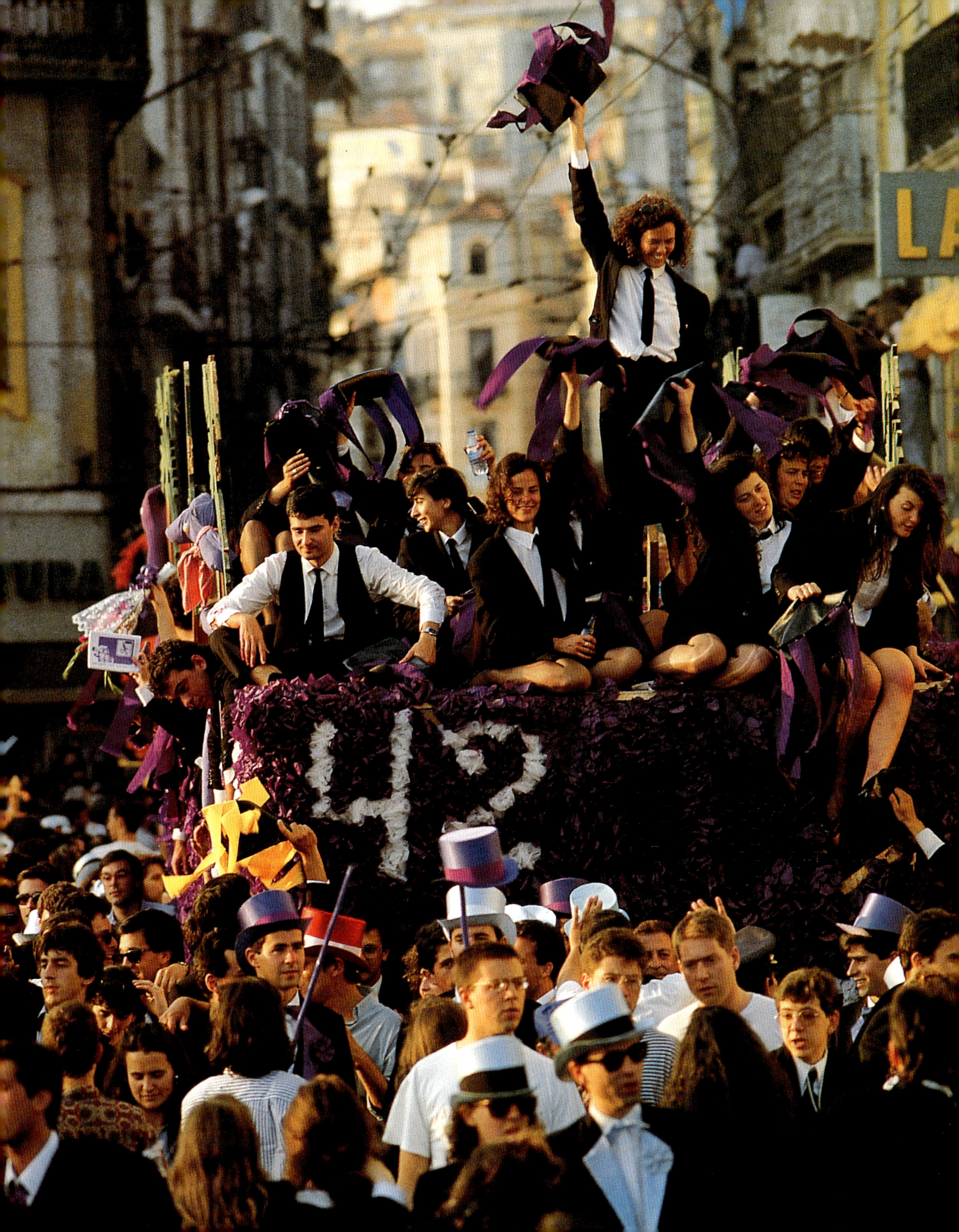
LA

The call of the ocean

108 *Life in Portugal has always been lived on the sea shores. The inland areas may have guaranteed refuge and food during invasions but the country's true wealth is the ocean. Ploughed by* moliceiros *and large fishing boats, whalers and merchant ships, caravels and galleons, the Atlantic created Portugal as a nation, when all the aspirations and hopes of the Portuguese people were placed in that great imperial adventure of colonialism.*

109 *Unmistakable in shape and colour, for years the* moliceiros *bore generations of fishermen along the coasts of Portugal. Today they are also a source of tourist wealth: the attractions of the Atlantic beaches now include these unusual boats hand-painted in bright colours by the fishermen themselves or, in some cases, by artist-craftsmen now specialised in the creation of new designs, mostly for the benefit of visitors. This minimal tourist exploitation of a traditional art should not be judged harshly: the recent "re-elaborations" are fruit of the same culture that produced the originals which – it must be stressed – still sail in Portuguese waters. A common feature of all the* moliceiros *is the curved or square high prow: this usually bears the most beautiful decorations, forming a sort of gaudy figure-head featuring attractive women and marine motifs.*

110

110-111 *In a country marching necessarily towards total integration with Europe, the produce of the sea is still one of Portugal's greatest treasures. The whalers and transoceanic fishing expeditions are no more, but mackerel, sardines and shell-fish still fully meet the domestic demand and are exported and appreciated all over Europe. The fishing fleet supplies part of Portuguese industry but, above all, fills the local restaurants with huge quantities of fresh produce.*

As a result, many Portuguese recipes feature fish dishes; in Lisbon as at Nazaré (where sardines are still dried in the sun at the water's edge), in Oporto and on the Algarve fish reign supreme: caldeirada *(fish soup), sole, turbot, bream, mullet as well as grilled sword-fish and hake. Another star of the Portuguese table is* bacalhau *or cod (there are said to be 365 ways of cooking it, one for every day of the year), usually* assado, fried, *or* cozido, *boiled and served with potatoes and a little olive oil. A must with every fish dish is of course a bottle of* vinho verde *produced in the Minho region or in the Douro valley.*

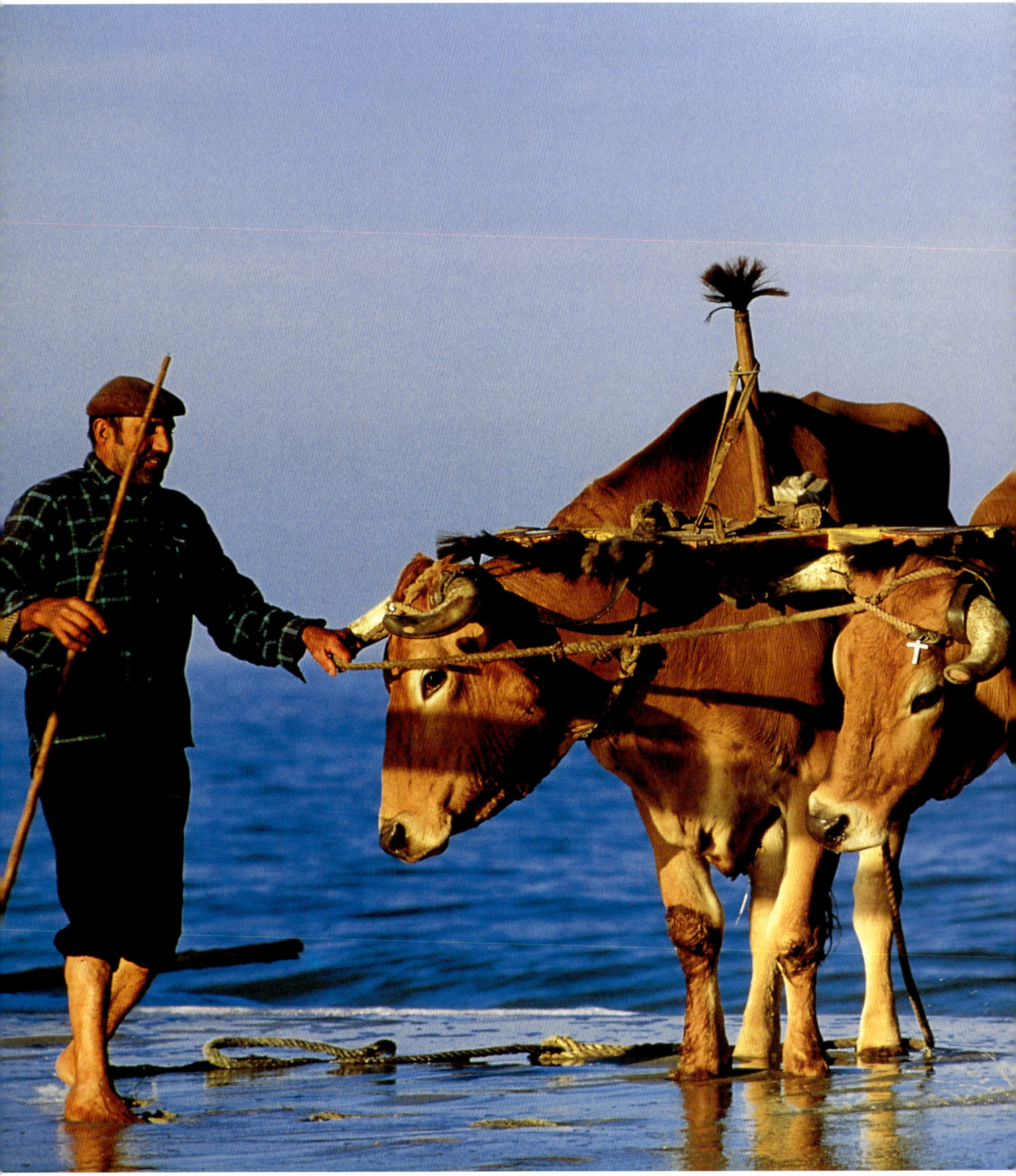

112-113 *Obliged by continental tradition to perform humble tasks in the fields, the ox has been redeemed on the Portuguese coasts. Having abandoned the fatigue of the plough, oxen in pairs aid the fishermen at their work. In particular they serve as motive power drawing the boats on shore after a fishing trip. Technological progress has come also to this edge of mainland Europe which, although reluctant before the boldest innovations, has nearly everywhere adopted internal combustion engines and jiggers. It is still possible, however, on some beaches of the Costa da Prata – at Aveiro (in the pictures) and at Nazaré – to admire the oxen at their ancient toil on the shore, proof that despite change Portugal is still a poor country bound to tradition.*

Feiras and folklore

114-115 *It is not unusual in Portugal to happen upon a fair or a festival, especially between May and October. As in many Latin countries, Portugal conserves great religious traditions, most mixed somewhat with local semi-pagan rituals that mix the stories of the saints with lay folklore and legend. The most famous festivals include the Dos Santos Populares in Lisbon (June), Nossa Senhora dos Navigantes at Cascais (Assumption Day), the Holy Trinity in Batalha (mid June), the Queima das Fitas in Coimbra (May), the Romaria de Nossa Senhora da Nazaré (September) the Dos Tabuleiros celebrations at Tomar (Whit Sunday), São Joao at Oporto (22nd/23rd June), Nossa Senhora da Agonia at Viana do Castelo (August). For each of these feiras out come the traditional costumes (red and white dresses with bodices, with lace and filigree jewellery for the women, white shirts with waistcoats and berets or hard-brimmed black hats for the men) and all go off to dance to the rhythm of tambourines and guitars.*

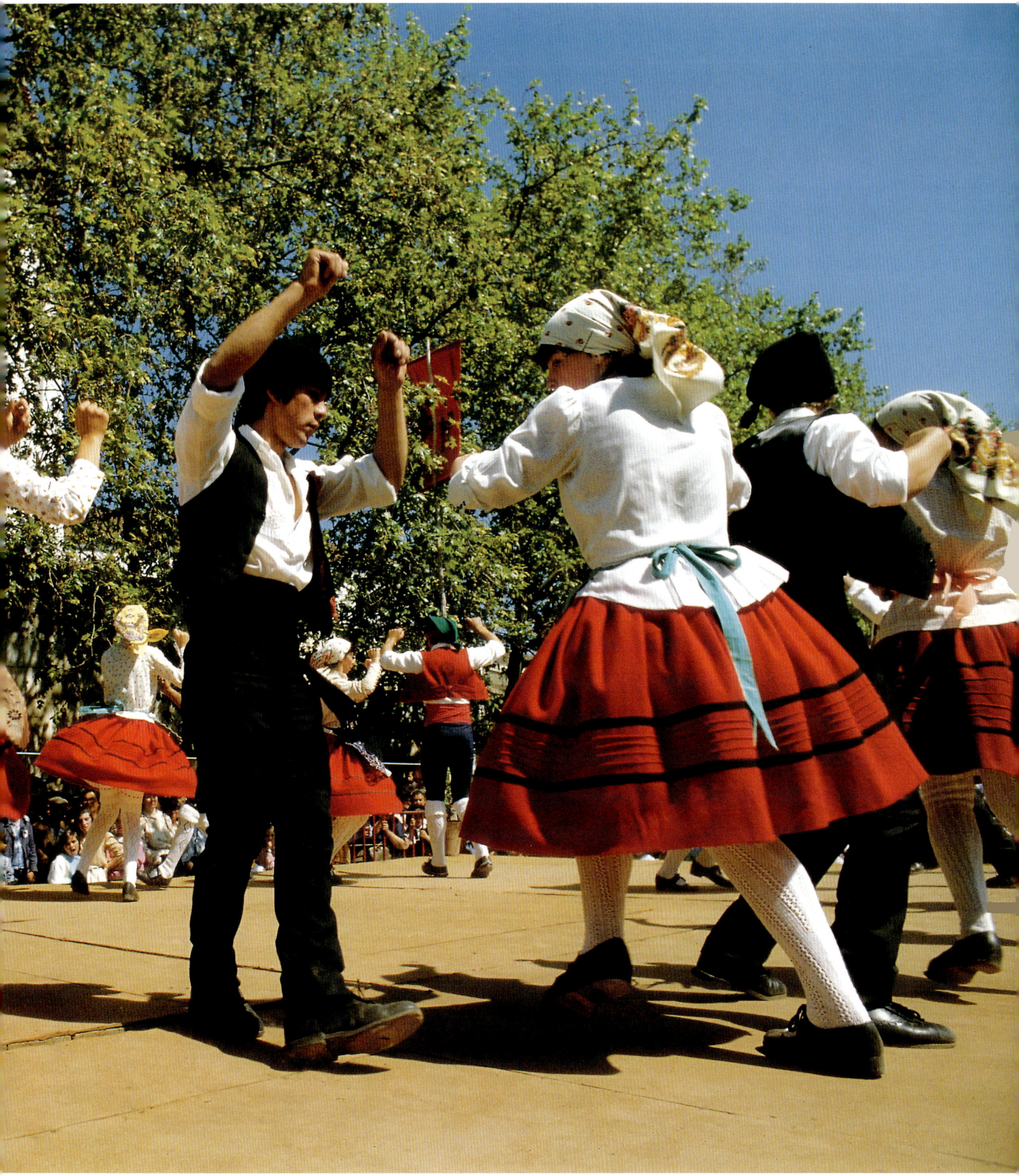

116-117 *Portuguese music and dancing, as too much of its literature, are little known outside the country. Yet the musical seasons, in Lisbon especially, are first class and generally well attended. A distinction must, however, be made between international and local music: the former is presented in the Teatro Nacional Opera House in Lisbon and at the Festival Internacional de Musica of Sintra; the latter is relegated to provincial festivals and a role of folk tradition in public places. This is not the case of* fado, *the Portuguese Blues played every evening in Coimbra, Oporto, Braga, and in the capital. Whether in small restaurants where they serve freshly-caught fish or in the countless Fado "houses", the guitar accompanies the melancholic song that originated perhaps in Brazil, perhaps in Africa, and embodies the deepest expression of the Portuguese soul,* saudade *(a mixture of home-sickness and emptiness).*

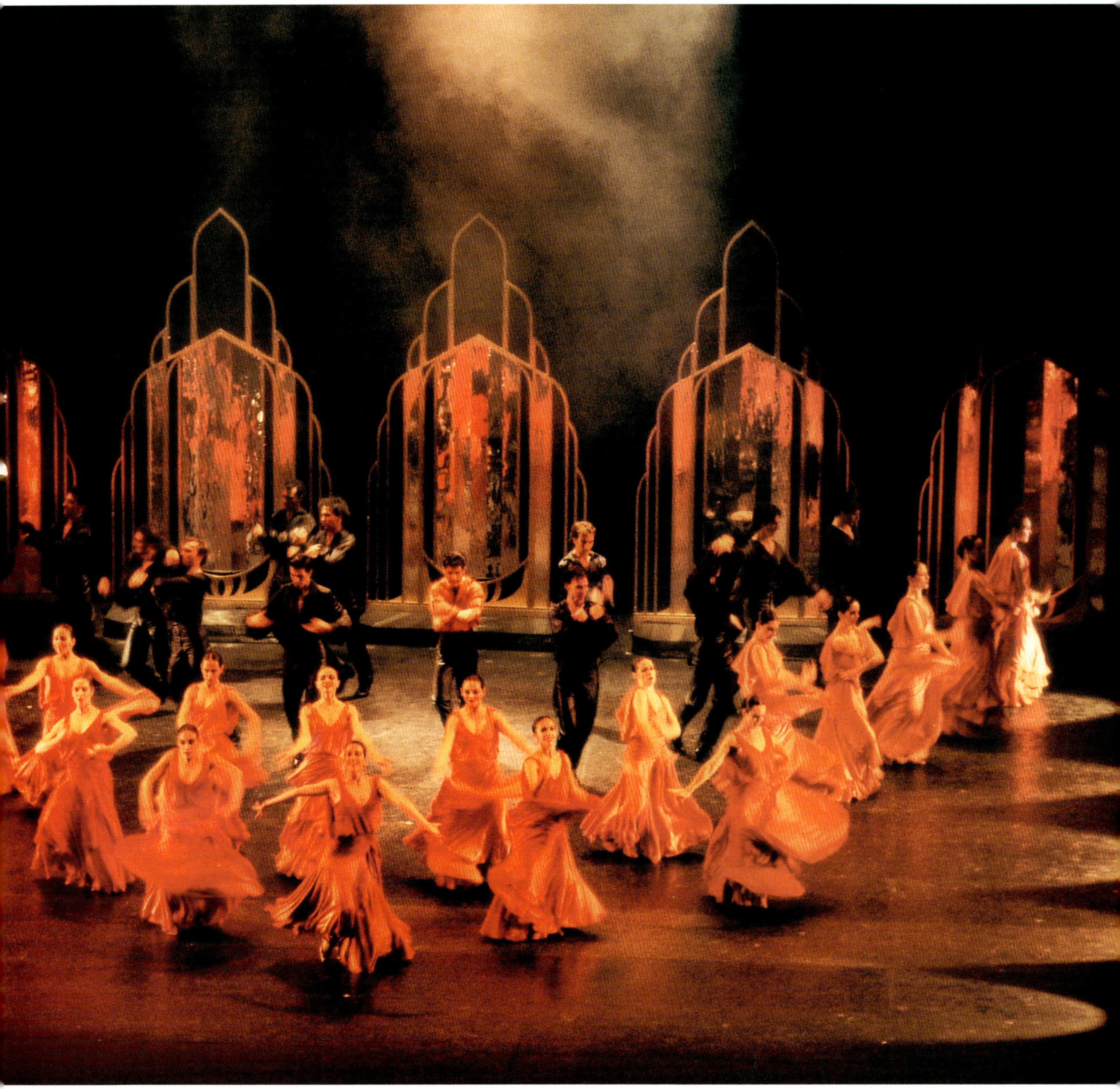

118 top right and left *The religious bond that unites all the Portuguese does not slacken even on the other side of the ocean as revealed by the festivals that animate the Azores several times a year, with the active participation of all the inhabitants. During the festival of Sant'Anna at São Miguel the congregation carry heavy wooden statues through the streets of Furnas (bottom). At Pico, for the Holy Spirit celebrations, the ancient custom of carrying bread in procession before its blessing lives on (top).*

118 bottom right *The greatest religious celebrations are those held in Braga, the cradle of Portuguese Catholicism. During Holy Week, the believers walk in procession on both Holy Thursday and Good Friday along the walls of the old Roman town, stopping at the* passos, *small altars set up along the way.*

119 *The most famous festival of Viana do Castelo, along the Costa Verde, is that of Nossa Senhora da Agonia. The climax of the event is organised for Saturday when a hoard of people in costume flood the streets accompanied by music and wine. Similar feeling is aroused for the celebrations of the Cross, during which the procession takes the form of a parade, with great local participation.*

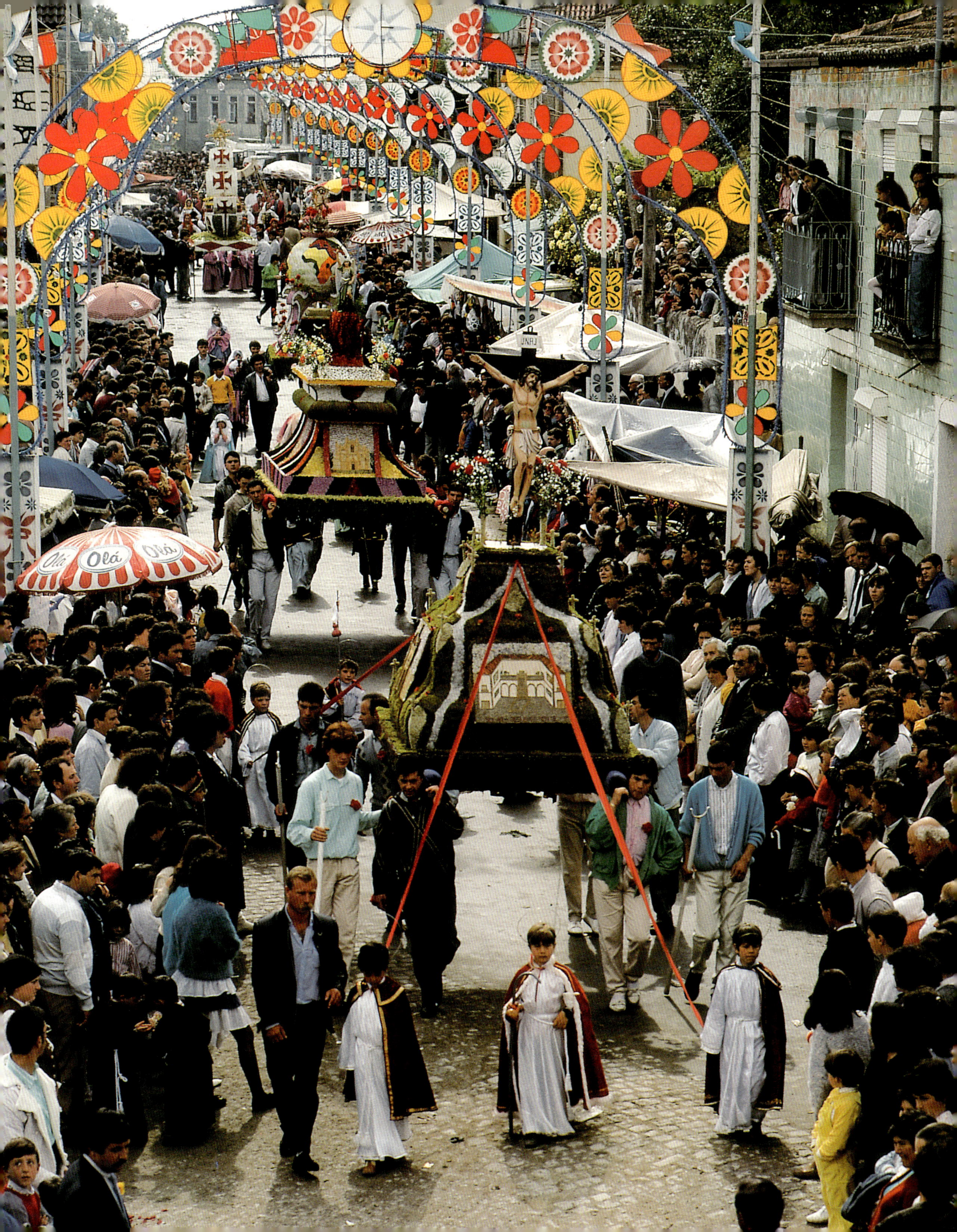
Olá
Olá
Olá

120-121 Touradas, *the Portuguese bullfights, are fascinating and spectacular but unlike those of Spain, not bloody. That is to say, even if the bull is injured it is not slaughtered. Its horns are bound with padding to reduce the danger and limit the risks of injury to the bullfighters, who are not only on foot, as in Spain, but on horseback too. The decision to make the* touradas *less violent events was taken following a serious accident in which count d'Arcos was killed during one: the king was deeply distressed by the death of a relative and issued a series of precautions to reduce accidents. Since then bulls and bullfighters have left the arena alive and, at the most, suffer the odd minor injury, cured in a few days. In contrast, the poetic vein of the* tourada *has been accentuated with magnificent costumes, sometimes original 18th-century ones with wig and three-pointed hat, and symbolic gestures (such as the fake killing of the bull with a flower in place of the sword).*

122-123 Portuguese golf courses are just as efficient, prestigious and technically valid as the best greens in Europe and the rest of the world. Particularly famous are those in the elegant suburbs of Oporto and Lisbon and on the Algarve, very green and often situated spectacularly above the sea.

121

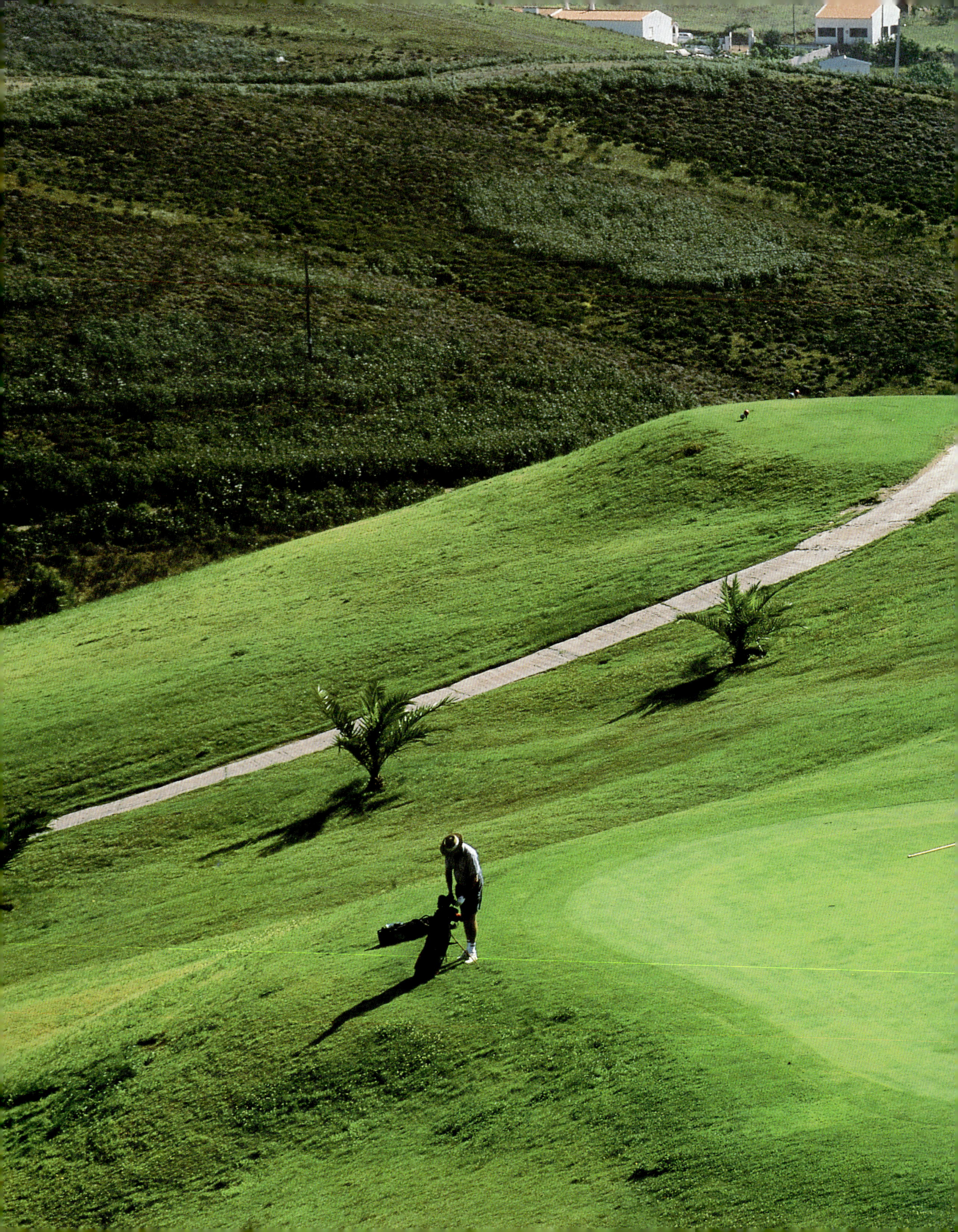

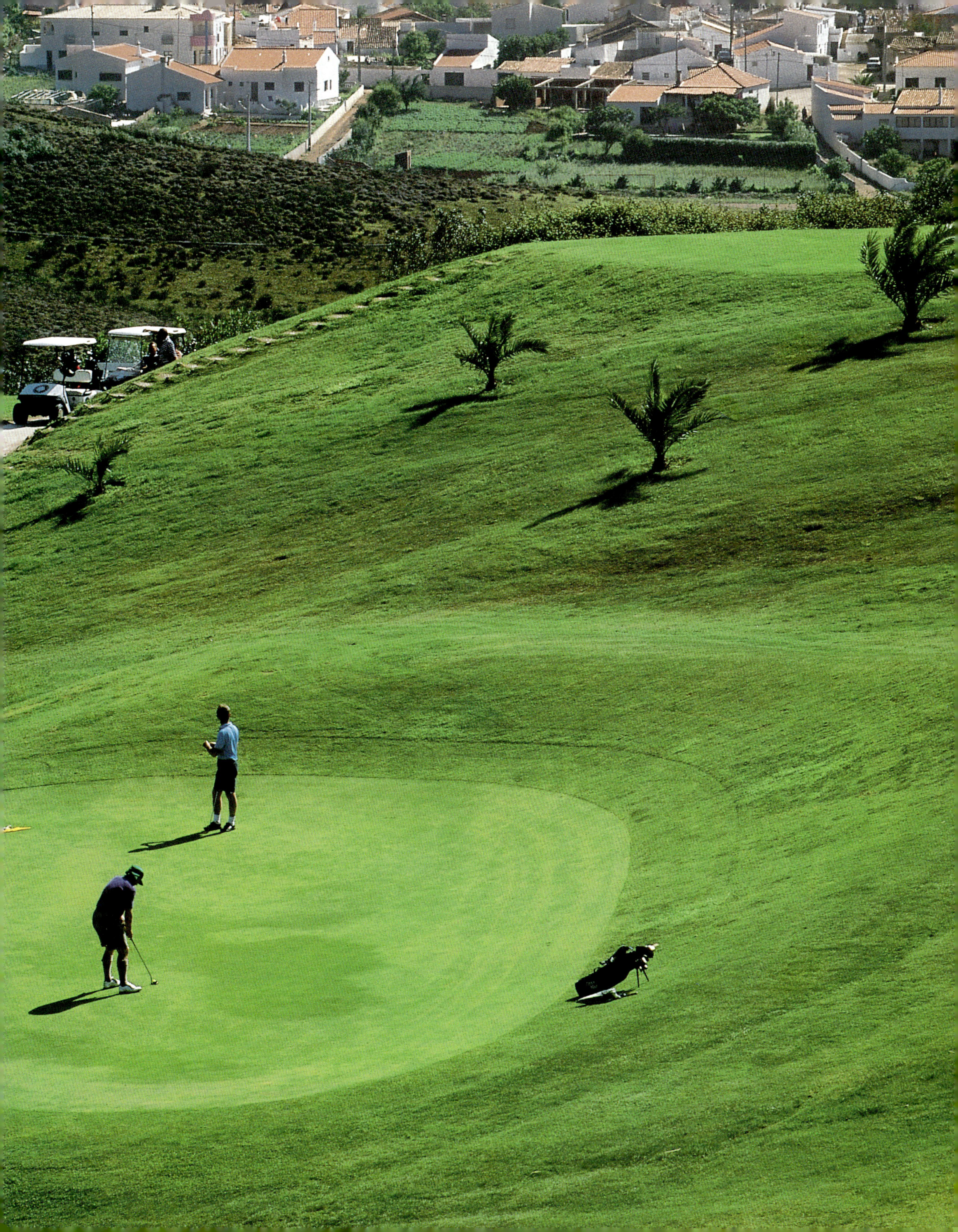

Coimbra, the roots of a new Portugal

124 *Coimbra, the first capital of Portugal, is now known as "the learned" for its crucial role in the country's cultural development. In its hands lie the Portuguese hopes of catching the train for Europe and leaving behind 200 years of economic decline and nearly 50 years of dictatorship. Coimbra is waging its hopes of becoming the nation's third metropolis on its university.*

Of mediaeval origin, it is one of the most prestigious on the continent, as is shown by the buildings used to house the offices, lecture rooms and, above all, the library, a Baroque gem containing more than 30,000 books plus a section devoted to rare mediaeval manuscripts. The heart of the university is the Sala dos Capelos (top left) where the most important moments of the academic year are lived.

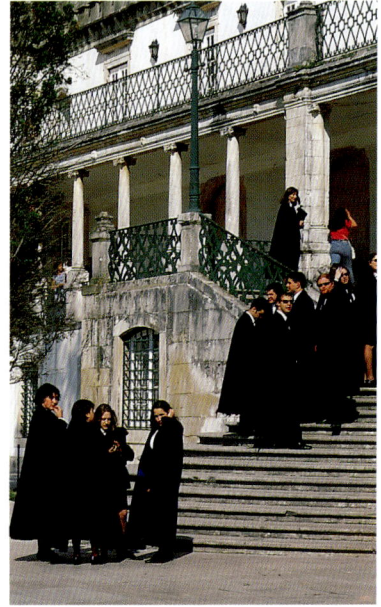

125 *Founded in 1290, the university of Coimbra had to share onus and honour with Lisbon until 1537 when it was reformed by King João III and turned into an independent academy. Since then it has constantly grown to become a leading European cultural pole. Although constant modernisation has given the faculty and academic institutes avant-garde facilities, Coimbra maintains certain age-old traditions that make it a "special" school. These range from the ceremonies for the start (in the picture) and end of the school year to formal graduations and the repúblicas.*

126-127 *The repúblicas are characteristic "hostels" run by the Coimbra university students themselves; grouped in communities of 15 or 20 they govern themselves in total freedom, sharing domestic duties, financial resources and academic experiences.*

128 *The image shows the spire and statue of the Redeemer, towering above the sanctuary of Fátima.*

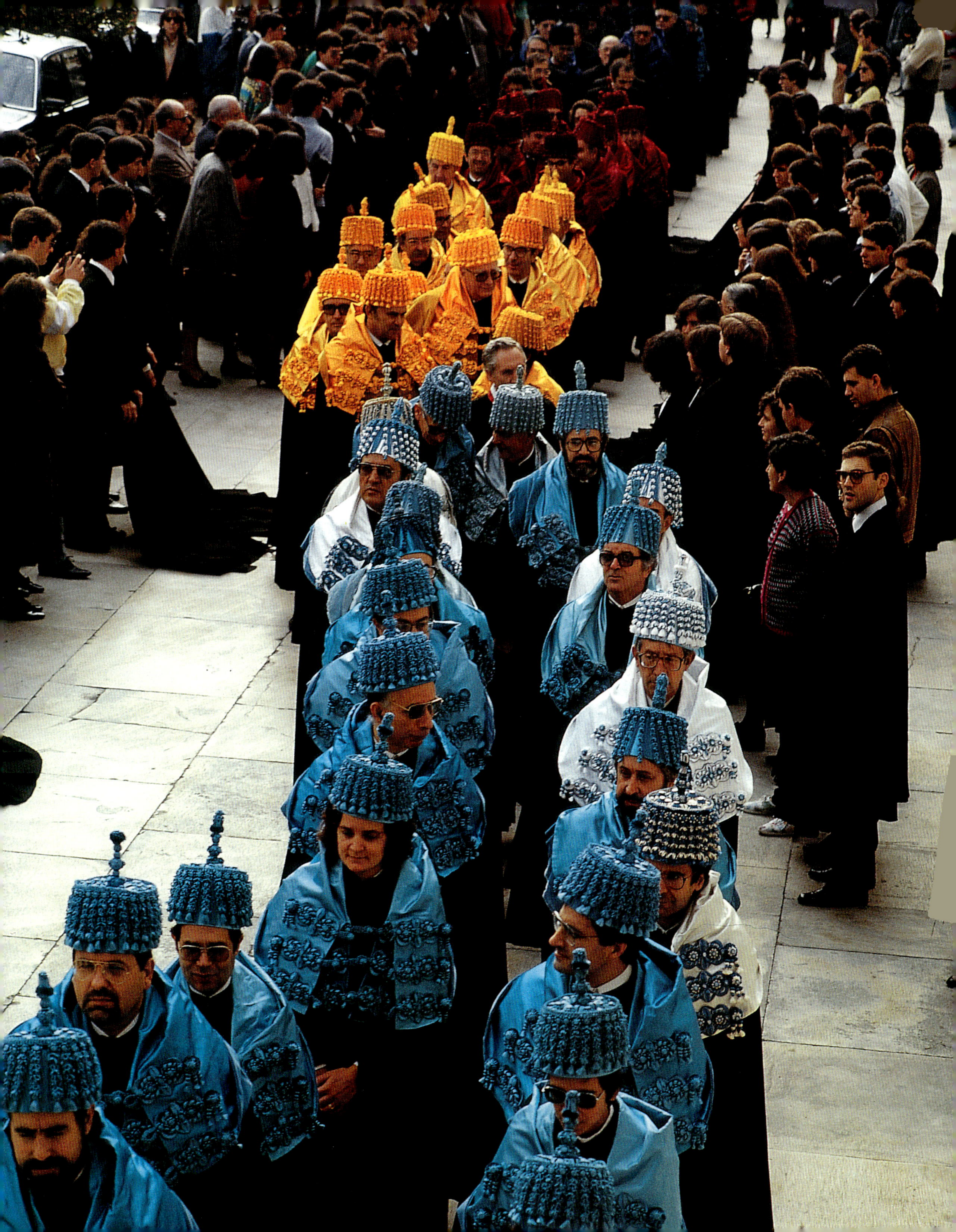

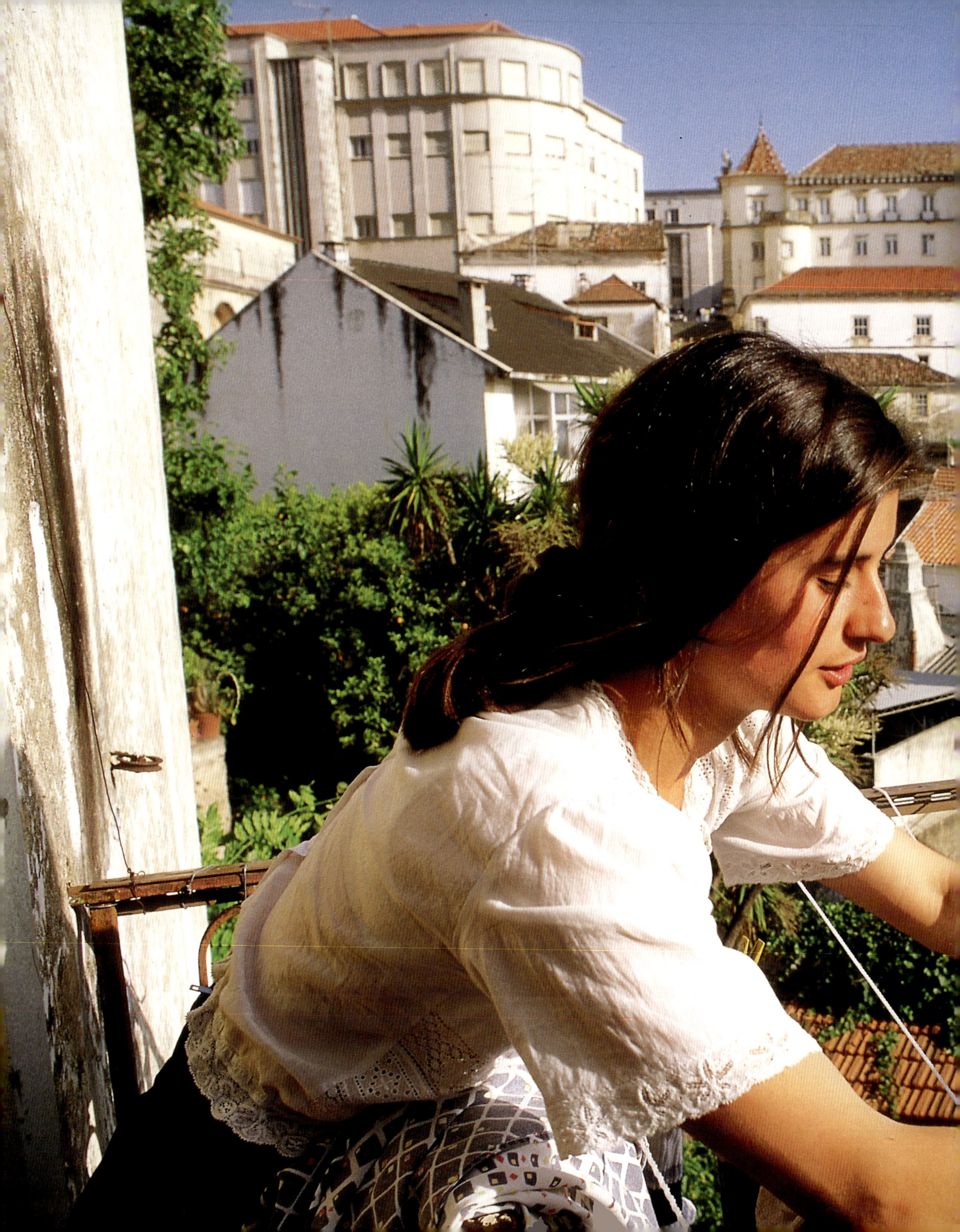

Illustration credits:

Antonio Attini / White Star: pages 30-31, 32-33, 68, 70 top, 70-71, 71, 72, 73, 75 top, 76 top, 76-77, 78, 79, 80, 81, 104 top, 104 centre left, 104 bottom, 105, 106 bottom, 114-115, 116, 117.

Giulio Veggi / White Star: pages 1, 2-3, 4-5, 6-7, 8, 9, 10 top right, 10 centre, 10 bottom, 16-17, 18, 22 top, 23, 24-25, 27, 28-29, 29, 34 bottom, 35, 36, 37, 40 top, 40-41, 42 left, 42-43, 46, 50-51, 52, 53, 54-55, 56, 57, 58-59, 69, 82, 83, 84-85, 85 top and centre, 86, 87, 89 top and centre, 90 centre right, 90 bottom, 92 top, 94, 95, 98, 99, 102, 103, 104 centre right, 109 bottom, 110 top right, 122-123, 124 top, 128.

Stefano Amantini / Atlantide: pages 46-47.

Bruno Barbier / Ag. Speranza: pages 114 top, 119, 121.

Bruno Barbier / Hémispheres: pages 12-13, 19, 40 bottom, 60-61, 89 bottom, 108, 114 bottom, 118 top, 120-121, 125.

Fausto Giaccone / Ag. Speranza: pages 106 top, 107, 118 bottom right, 124 bottom, 126-127.

Fausto Giaccone / SIE: pages 42 right, 114-115.

François Gohier / Ag. Speranza: page 63 bottom.

David W. Hamilton / Image Bank: page 45 bottom.

Franck Lechenet / Hémisperes: pages 14-15, 62 centre.

Marco Leopardi / SIE: pages 48-49.

W. Louvet / Ag. Visa: pages 109 top, 112, 113.

Marco Mairani / Focus Team: page 45 top.

Jose Manuel / Image Bank: pages 22 bottom, 90 top.

Orbassano / Focus Team: pages 110 top left, 111 left.

Jean Charles Pinheira: pages 34 top, 38, 44-45, 61 top, 62 top, 62-63, 64 top, 70 bottom, 74-75, 75 bottom, 76 centre and bottom, 85 bottom, 92 bottom, 93, 100, 101, 110 bottom, 118 bottom left.

Stefano Scatà / Image Bank: page 65 bottom.

Schinco / Focus Team: page 11.

Tavanti / Focus Team: pages 20-21, 65 top.

Angelo Tondini / Focus Team: pages 10 top left, 45 centre.

Yvan Travert / Ag. Speranza: pages 39 bottom, 64 bottom, 66-67, 88-89, 96-97.

Pawel Wysocki / Hémispheres: pages 39 top, 90 centre left, 90-91.

C. Alberto Zabert / Realy Easy Star: pages 62 bottom, 111 right.